CW00349994

Hour-Long Shakespeare

Volume II

Romeo and Juliet
Macbeth
Julius Caesar

Abridged by
Matthew Jenkinson

First published 2015
by John Catt Educational Ltd,
12 Deben Mill Business Centre, Old Maltings Approach,
Melton, Woodbridge IP12 1BL
Tel: +44 (0) 1394 389850
Fax: +44 (0) 1394 386893
Email: enquiries@johncatt.com
Website: www.johncatt.com

Opinions expressed in this publication are those of the contributors
and are not necessarily those of the publishers or the editors.
We cannot accept responsibility for any errors or omissions.

All performing rights of these adaptations are fully protected
and permission to perform them must be obtained in advance,
by sending the following information to John Catt Educational
(enquiries@johncatt.com or 12 Deben Mill Business Centre, Melton,
Woodbridge, IP12 1BL, United Kingdom): play title; place of
performance; number of performances; seating capacity; ticket prices;
not-for-profit or for-profit organisation; performance dates. Any
advertising material for the performance(s) should include the text
'abridged by Matthew Jenkinson in the *Hour-Long Shakespeare* series'.

ISBN: 978 1 909717 49 7

Set and designed by Theoria Design Ltd
www.theoriadesign.com

Printed and bound in Great Britain
by The Charlesworth Press

Contents

And so, from hour to hour, we ripe and ripe ...

- *As You Like It* (II, vii, 26)

FOREWORD

Most editions of Shakespeare are difficult to read. Apart from the language itself — so challenging to a newbie — they are notorious for tiny print, complicated footnotes and impenetrable intros. It's almost as if their makers don't actually *want* children and young people to enjoy Shakespeare. This edition is different. *Hour-Long Shakespeare* skilfully abridges Shakespeare's plays to emphasise the best bits (and give everyone a decent part), and the text itself is big, clear and easy to read.

When I got hold of the first volume, I quickly realised that *Hour-Long Shakespeare* is a great resource for schools and colleges. I also decided that every home should have one. After all, you can own a *Complete Works of Shakespeare* (weighing a ton, microscopic print, almost a million words) that just gathers dust on the family bookshelf, or you can try a book that makes it simple to have some fun performing Shakespeare as a family, in your own home (or, even better, garden).

Which brings me to this second volume of the *Hour-Long Shakespeare* series. Full of gobsmacking events, unforgettable characters and immortal lines, *Romeo and Juliet*, *Macbeth* and *Julius Caesar* are three of Shakespeare's best and 'easiest' plays. Any young person with these three plays under their belt will be in a great place to start taking on the world. But most of all, Shakespeare is meant to be enjoyed. This book will enable you to have a laugh and make some noise while getting blown away by the guy from Stratford who, after four hundred years, is still the best writer in town.

Pat Reid
Editor of *Shakespeare Magazine*

SHAKESPEARE ABBREVIATED

This impressive and practicable collection of shortened Shakespeares is only the latest expression of a tradition which dates all the way back to the working practices of Shakespeare's own company and to the pedagogical habits of Shakespeare's own schooldays. Shakespeare usually delivered scripts up to twenty per cent longer than those provided by fellow-playwrights of the time, and they were generally trimmed for performance, presumably with his own assistance. His authorial draft of *Hamlet*, for instance, the version printed as the second quarto in 1603, was 3,800 lines long, but the play had been reduced to a more practicable 3,600-line acting version by the time the First Folio went to press in 1623. Even so, the English players who were already touring the Baltic and Germany at around this time preferred to use the rougher, simpler script printed as the first quarto in 1603, not least because it is only 2,200 lines long.

Shakespeare's plays have always expanded and contracted to suit available performance times and available casts: during the English civil wars, when the playhouses were closed and theatrical performances could take place only surreptitiously and unofficially in taverns and fairground booths, *Henry IV, Part 1* was shortened to become *The Bouncing Knight* (consisting solely of those scenes dealing with the highway robbery and its comic aftermath), *A Midsummer Night's Dream* became *The Merry Conceited Humours of Bottom the Weaver* (by losing most of the scenes dealing only with the Athenian lovers), and *Hamlet* dwindled to *The Grave-Makers* – just the gravediggers' scene. At least the Prince still got to pose with a skull.

As theatres experimented with ever more elaborate scenery, requiring ever-longer scene changes, and as actors flirted with ever longer naturalistic pauses in their delivery, so the history of Shakespeare's texts in performance from the Restoration to the early twentieth century was primarily a history of progressive cutting. Acting editions from the 1670s onwards suggested which lines could be omitted from stage performances, if the play was 'too long to be acted upon the stage'. By the end of the Victorian period the lines marked for omission in the playhouses sometimes outnumbered the ones left in. They have certainly continued to do so in the medium that soon took over the mass audiences and many of the conventions of the nineteenth-century stage, namely the cinema. Generally restricted to a duration of between an hour and a half and two hours, and always inclined to reduce speech in favour of visuals, film versions of Shakespeare have usually retained much less of Shakespeare's writing than do the hour-long acting scripts published here. Although Sir Kenneth Branagh appeased his artistic conscience by making a film of *Hamlet* which conflates both the second quarto and Folio texts to produce a version longer than either, for instance, he prepared a ninety-minute edit for commercial release too, and his film of *Love's Labours Lost* uses less than a third of the original play's dialogue.

Alongside this pragmatic tradition of simply making Shakespeare's plays shorter for commercial purposes, though, there has been from the first a tradition of shortening them for educational performance, and it is a tradition which has often produced much more interesting results. Shakespeare himself would have taken part in classroom performances of edited Latin plays at his grammar school in Stratford, and his own plays soon participated themselves in this humanist tradition of theatre-in-education.

In the autumn of 2014 a copy of the 1623 First Folio was discovered in the library of the Jesuit seminary at St Omer near Calais, to which English Catholics sent their sons to be educated in the days when Anglicanism still held a monopoly back home. Some plays are missing entirely (as if they have been excised so as to be more portable when used as scripts?), while some that remain have been marked up with school performance in mind, probably during the later 1620s and 1630s. The Jesuits disapproved of thespian cross-dressing, and hence instead of having boys play female roles they either cut Shakespeare's female characters or changed them into men – throughout the St Omer copy of *Henry IV, Part 1*, for instance, the Hostess (Mistress

Quickly) is simply altered by repeated strokes of the pen on her speech prefixes to become the Host (presumably, Mr Quickly). Hotspur's wife Lady Percy disappears, and Falstaff speaks only of 'fellows' and never of 'wenches.' As well as keeping expatriate students in touch with at least an edited version of their own vernacular culture, these Catholic educational performances of abbreviated Shakespeare – the earliest known school performances of Shakespeare plays – produced a distinctive and lasting theatrical culture of their own. Surviving original plays written by seventeenth-century masters for performance by St Omer schoolboys, for instance, are of noticeably high literary quality and are permeated with allusions to Shakespeare, while later graduates from these drama-saturated Catholic seminaries abroad included John Philip Kemble, perhaps the finest Shakespearean actor (and abbreviator) of the Romantic period.

Perhaps as a result of his own formative experiences at school, Kemble became an admirer of the visionary grammar-school teacher Richard Valpy (1754-1836), who produced such expertly-cut versions of Shakespeare for performance by his pupils in Reading that many were published and one, his redaction of *King John*, was even acted at the Theatre Royal, Covent Garden, in 1803. Like the Jesuit seminarists before him, Valpy realized that when altering Shakespeare for a cast of non-transvestite schoolboys he could work much more readily from the history plays than from the comedies and tragedies, not least because not only do they tend to sideline their women, but they already contain many diverse male roles of approximately equal size and prominence. A stern moralist, Valpy also saw in the abbreviation of Shakespeare an opportunity to improve him: 'When the First Part of King Henry the Fourth was played at Reading School,' he wrote,

> it was sufficient to curtail some tedious pages, and to omit some exceptionable expressions. In the Second Part it was absolutely necessary to do more. This play in the original is disfigured not only with indelicate speeches, but with characters that cannot now be tolerated on a public theatre.

Less censorious educational acting versions of Shakespeare since Valpy's have included the forty-five-minute redactions performed in a small replica of an Elizabethan playhouse at the Chicago World's Fair of 1933, which are said to have inspired the young Sam Wanamaker, subsequent founder of the replica Globe in London; and the ingenious shortened versions of the comedies, their surviving roles carefully tailored to approximately equal length, in which the Swedish educator Kiki Lindell casts her literature undergraduates as a means of simultaneously teaching them drama, English, and Shakespeare.

Matthew Jenkinson's careful alterations of some of Shakespeare's most important plays – which cunningly avoid the risks of the star system by involving their whole casts in speeches reassigned as choric, thereby underlining the continuity between Shakespeare's plays and the classical drama he had himself learned at school – may give us less than fifty per cent of each play's lines, but they convey far more than that percentage of each play's theatrical power. Moreover, they belong one hundred per cent to the highest traditions of both teaching and performing Shakespeare's plays.

Professor Michael Dobson
Director of the Shakespeare Institute, Stratford-upon-Avon, and
Professor of Shakespeare Studies, University of Birmingham

General Introduction

This book consists of reduced versions of three of Shakespeare's most famous tragedies: *Romeo and Juliet, Macbeth* and *Julius Caesar*. It is not a book for purists, nor for those seeking a study text. It is, instead, for those who wish to perform (or read) a Shakespeare play, but do not have the time or resources to stage (or read) a full-length version. Without an interval, and with some musical interludes, each of these plays takes about an hour to perform. Naturally, cutting out almost two-thirds of each original play means that many speeches are shorter than in the original, some sections of plot have been removed, and whole characters sometimes have been excised altogether. But the texts have been edited to retain the essence of the central plots, to give a sense of the principal characters, as well as a taste of Shakespeare's original language. The integrity of this language has been preserved. The lines are, in general, as printed in the First Folio of 1623, with, where appropriate, some modernized spellings, and capital letters silently lowered. The words of the original plays have not been changed; there are just fewer of them. Act and scene numbers do not always correspond to those in the original texts, however, as some scenes have disappeared altogether, and others have been moved to aid the overall sense of the abridged versions.

The casting of the plays has been engineered for the greatest flexibility. There are usually approximately twenty named parts, each with a different level of challenge. If someone wishes to be involved in a Shakespeare production, but is not confident about learning lots of lines or being on the stage for too long, there is a part for them. Equally, if someone wishes to take on a much larger role like Juliet, Romeo, Macbeth, Brutus, Cassius or Mark Antony, there is a part for them too. And, of course, there are plenty of medium-engagement roles for those in the middle.

The Chorus device is used throughout the plays. This narrator-style method enables the Chorus to provide excerpts from otherwise-excised sections of the plays, to take on characters like Roman citizens in *Julius Caesar* or witches in *Macbeth*, or to provide a commentary on the unfolding drama. The Chorus device also aids flexibility in casting. It is possible to have just one individual narrating the Chorus part, or several actors can take the Chorus lines in turn. When these hour-long versions were staged originally, between fifteen and twenty Chorus members were used, sitting behind the audience 'in the round', taking each line in turn. In addition to enhancing the atmosphere of the performance, this also enables the Chorus to have the script in front of them, catering for those who wish to engage with Shakespeare's language and the production as a whole, but who do not yet feel confident enough to learn lines or perform on the main stage. In this edition, Shakespeare's original lineation sometimes has been changed, to provide more natural line breaks, should the production include more than one Chorus member.

This edition includes pointers for 'musical interludes' or 'battle sounds'. The precise natures of the interludes are, of course, up to the directors of individual productions. The abridged version of *Romeo and Juliet* in this volume includes a musical interlude as the Capulet ball gets underway. Any Renaissance dance music would provide the appropriate atmosphere. Nino Rota's score for Franco Zefferelli's 1968 film of *Romeo and Juliet* may also provide some inspiration. Battle sounds can be created by Chorus members hitting the backs of their chairs with drumsticks. Equally, directors may wish to amplify pre-recorded battle sounds: whatever works in the particular context of each production.

There is also great flexibility in the age range of those who can be involved in the hour-long productions. The original cast members of these abridged plays were between eleven and thirteen years old. They demonstrated that this age group really can engage with, act in, and enjoy, Shakespeare's plays. While it would probably be rare for younger children to attempt these edited versions, there is of course no upper age limit. One of the best ways to learn about Shakespeare is to perform one of his plays. Even if you only have a couple of lines, you become immersed in the language and begin to encounter and understand core themes and plots. It is intended that these scripts will help in that learning process.

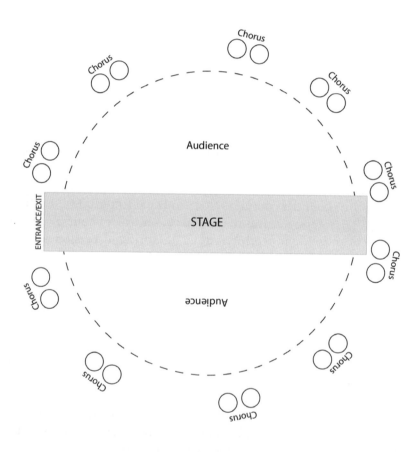

Romeo and Juliet

INTRODUCTION

If the speed at which Romeo and Juliet meet, fall in love, then die is implausible in Shakespeare's original play, then it is verging on the ridiculous in this hour-long version. Then again, falling in love at first sight is a rapid process. The precise manner in which the ill-fated lovers meet, marry, and take their own lives has been retained in this abridged version. There are just fewer lines to dilute the increasingly-fraught tragedy, and no scenes whatsoever with musicians or cooks to provide something resembling comic relief. The Chorus delivers Shakespeare's famous prologue, but it is also used to deliver some of the longer speeches, including Mercutio's 'Queen Mab' mockery and Friar Laurence's not-so-brief explanation towards the end of the play as to how the tragedy has unfolded. The Nurse in the original play is famously a loquacious gossip; in this adaptation she has to get to the point rather more quickly.

SYNOPSIS

The Chorus introduces *Romeo and Juliet* by informing us of a long-standing feud between two esteemed Verona families: the Montagues and the Capulets. We are told that the offspring of these families are fated to take their own lives, having fallen in love. Two members of the Capulet household, Sampson and Gregory, are walking Verona's streets, discussing the Montague/Capulet feud, which is reignited when Sampson insults his foes by biting his thumb at them. Tybalt, a Capulet, enters the fray and continues the skirmish, despite attempts by Benvolio to keep the peace. The heads of the families appear, but so does the Prince, who commands the Montagues and Capulets to drop their weapons and to keep the peace, 'on pain of death'.

A love-sick Romeo arrives and tells Benvolio that the object of his affections has chosen to live a chaste life. Benvolio's solution is simple: to forget about her and 'examine other beauties'. Meanwhile, Paris informs Capulet that he wishes to marry Capulet's daughter, Juliet. Capulet is sceptical at first, but invites Paris to a feast at the Capulet house to try to woo her. Capulet sends out a servant to invite others to the feast, but the servant cannot read the invitation. He bumps into Romeo and Benvolio, who read the invitation on the servant's behalf, thus finding out about the Capulet feast. Benvolio spies this as the perfect opportunity for Romeo to see other beauties.

Lady Capulet and the Nurse inform Juliet of Paris's desire to make her his wife. Juliet protests that she is too young to think of marriage, though she agrees to meet Paris at the Capulet feast. Romeo remains lovesick and Mercutio mocks him (with the help of the Chorus) for his dreaminess. The Capulet feast begins and Romeo attends, though Tybalt spots him and wishes to fight him as he takes this appearance as an insult. Capulet implores Tybalt to keep the peace, but Tybalt resolves not to forget Romeo's intrusion. Romeo and Juliet meet, fall in love, and resolve to marry the following day.

Romeo informs Friar Laurence of his new-found love. Friar Laurence agrees to marry Romeo and Juliet, as it will unite the Capulet and Montague families and hopefully end their quarrel. Romeo sends word of the marriage plans to Juliet, via her Nurse. Romeo and Juliet are married. Tybalt challenges Romeo to a duel, but Romeo refuses to fight as (unknown to Tybalt) they are now family. Mercutio fights in Romeo's stead, but Tybalt stabs him under Romeo's arm. Romeo is angered by Mercutio's death, and kills Tybalt. The Prince exiles Romeo.

The Nurse returns to Juliet and, after some confusion, informs her that Romeo has killed Tybalt and has therefore been banished. Juliet grieves for Tybalt, but soon resolves that Romeo only killed Tybalt in self-defence, and Romeo's banishment is cause for greater lament. Friar Laurence tells Romeo to stay in Mantua until he can find an opportunity to pacify the Prince and pave the way for Romeo's return to Verona. Meanwhile, Capulet arranges for Juliet to marry Paris after all – and very soon. After a final meeting with Juliet, Romeo leaves for Mantua.

Juliet is told of the new plan for her to marry Paris, which she refuses to do. Juliet asks Friar Laurence how she can get out of the marriage; she threatens to stab herself otherwise. Friar Laurence devises a plan: the night before her wedding to Paris, Juliet is to drink a potion that will make her appear dead. The Capulets will place her body in the family vault, where she will awake after forty-two hours, to be met by Romeo who will spirit her away. After some angst and uncertainty, Juliet takes the potion. Juliet is found 'dead' and her body is indeed taken to the Capulet vault. However, the letter Friar Laurence has sent to Romeo to inform him of this plan is not delivered. Balthasar arrives in Mantua instead, and tells Romeo that Juliet is dead. Romeo buys a poison from an impoverished apothecary and resolves to use that poison so he can die alongside Juliet.

Romeo returns to Verona and encounters Paris by the Capulet vault. The two fight and Paris is killed. Romeo lies by Juliet and drinks his poison. Friar Laurence arrives at the vault too late and is scared away by some noise. He implores Juliet to follow him, but she refuses. Instead, she tries to take some poison from Romeo's lips. When this does not work, she stabs herself. The bodies of Paris, Romeo and Juliet are discovered. The Prince asks for clarification of what has happened; the Chorus summarises all that has occurred. The Capulets and Montagues resolve to end their feud: the Montagues will raise a statue in honour of Juliet, the Capulets in honour of Romeo.

CAST

(in order of appearance)

Chorus
Sampson
Gregory
Abraham
Balthasar
Benvolio
Tybalt
Capulet
Lady Capulet
Montague
Lady Montague
Prince
Romeo
Paris
Servant
Nurse
Juliet
Mercutio
Friar Laurence
Apothecary
Friar John

PROLOGUE

CHORUS
Two households, both alike in dignity,
In fair Verona, where we lay our scene,
From ancient grudge break to new mutiny,
Where civil blood makes civil hands unclean.
From forth the fatal loins of these two foes
A pair of star-cross'd lovers take their life;
Whose misadventured piteous overthrows
Do with their death bury their parents' strife.
The fearful passage of their death-mark'd love,
And the continuance of their parents' rage,
Which, but their children's end, nought could remove,
Is now the hour's traffic of our stage;
The which if you with patient ears attend,
What here shall miss, our toil shall strive to mend.

Act 1, Scene 1

A public place in Verona

Enter SAMPSON and GREGORY of the house of Capulet

SAMPSON
Gregory: o'my word, we'll not carry coals.

GREGORY
No, for then we should be colliers.

SAMPSON
I mean, if we be in choler, we'll draw.

GREGORY
Ay, while you live, draw your neck out o'th'collar.

SAMPSON
I strike quickly, being mov'd.

GREGORY
But thou art not quickly mov'd to strike.

SAMPSON
A dog of the house of Montague moves me.

GREGORY
The quarrel is between our masters and us their men.

Enter ABRAHAM and BALTHASAR

SAMPSON
'Tis all one,
Draw thy tool, here comes
Two of the house of the Montagues.
I will bite my thumb at them,
Which is a disgrace to them, if they bear it.

ABRAHAM
Do you bite your thumb at us, sir?

SAMPSON
I do bite my thumb, sir.

ABRAHAM
Do you bite your thumb at us, sir?

SAMPSON
[Aside to GREGORY] Is the law of our side, if I say ay?

GREGORY
No.

SAMPSON
No sir, I do not bite my thumb at you, sir: but
I bite my thumb, sir.

GREGORY
Do you quarrel, sir?

ABRAHAM
Quarrel sir? No, sir.

SAMPSON
If you do, sir, I am for you: I serve as good a man as you.

BALTHASAR
No better.

SAMPSON
Yes, better.

They draw then fight. Battle sounds. Enter BENVOLIO

BENVOLIO
Part, fools, you know not what you do.

Beats down their swords. Enter TYBALT

TYBALT
What art thou drawn among these heartless
Hinds? Turn thee Benvolio, look upon thy death.

BENVOLIO
I do but keep the peace.

TYBALT
What, drawn, and talk of peace? I hate the word
As I hate hell, all Montagues, and thee.

They fight. Enter CAPULET and LADY CAPULET

CAPULET
What noise is this? Give me my long sword, ho.
Old Montague is come,
And flourishes his blade in spite of me.

Enter MONTAGUE and LADY MONTAGUE

MONTAGUE
Thou villain Capulet.

LADY MONTAGUE
Thou shalt not stir a foot to seek a foe.

Enter PRINCE

PRINCE
Rebellious subjects, enemies to peace,
Throw your mistemper'd weapons to the ground,
And hear the sentence of your moved prince.
Three civil brawls, bred of an airy word,
By thee old Capulet and Montague,
Have thrice disturb'd the quiet of our streets.
If ever you disturb our streets again,
Your lives shall pay the forfeit of the peace.
You Capulet shall go along with me,
And Montague come you this afternoon,
To know our further pleasure in this case:
On pain of death, all men depart.

Exeunt all except BENVOLIO. Enter ROMEO

ROMEO
O me. What fray was here?

BENVOLIO
Good morrow, cousin.

ROMEO
Is the day so young?

BENVOLIO
But new struck nine.

ROMEO
Ay me, sad hours seem long.

BENVOLIO
What sadness lengthens Romeo's hours?

ROMEO
Not having that, which having, makes them short.

BENVOLIO
In love?

ROMEO
Out.

BENVOLIO
Of love?

ROMEO
Out of her favour, where I am in love.

BENVOLIO
Alas, that love, so gentle in his view,
Should be so tyrannous and rough in proof.

ROMEO
Alas that love, whose view is muffled still,
Should without eyes, see pathways to his will:
O brawling love, O loving hate,
O any thing, of nothing first created:
O heavy lightness, serious vanity,
Love is a smoke raised with the fume of sighs.

BENVOLIO
Tell me in sadness, who is that you love.

ROMEO
In sadness, cousin, I do love a woman.
But in strong proof of chastity well arm'd:
From love's weak childish bow, she lives unharm'd.

BENVOLIO
Be rul'd by me, forget to think of her
By giving liberty unto thine eyes,
Examine other beauties.

ROMEO
Show me a mistress that is passing fair,
What doth her beauty serve but as a note
Where I may read who pass'd that passing fair?
Farewell, thou canst not teach me to forget.

BENVOLIO
I'll pay that doctrine, or else die in debt.

Exeunt

Act 1, Scene 2

A Street

Enter CAPULET, PARIS and SERVANT

PARIS
Now my lord, what say you to my suit?

CAPULET
My child is yet a stranger in the world,
She hath not seen the change of fourteen years.

PARIS
Younger than she, are happy mothers made.

CAPULET
And too soon marr'd are those so early made:
Woo her, gentle Paris, get her heart,
My will to her consent, is but a part;
This night I hold an old accustom'd feast,
Whereto I have invited many a guest,
Such as I love, and you among the store.

To SERVANT, giving a paper

Go sirrah find those persons out,
Whose names are written there, and to them say,
My house and welcome, on their pleasure stay.

Exeunt CAPULET and PARIS

SERVANT
I am sent to find those persons whose names are here
Writ, and can never find what names the writing
Person hath here writ. I must to the learned.

Enter BENVOLIO and ROMEO

I pray sirs can you read?

ROMEO
Ay, if I know the letters and the language.

Reads

"Signior Martino and his wife and daughter;
Mercutio and his brother Valentine; mine
Uncle Capulet, his wife and daughters; my fair niece
Rosaline; Livia; Signior Valentio, and his cousin
Tybalt, Lucio and the lively Helena."
Whither should they come?

SERVANT
To supper; my master is the great rich Capulet,
And if you be not of the house of Montagues,
I pray come and crush a cup of wine.

Exit

BENVOLIO
At this same ancient feast of Capulet's
Sups the fair Rosaline, whom thou so loves:
Go thither and with unattainted eye,
Compare her face with some that I shall show,
And I will make thee think thy swan a crow.

ROMEO
I'll go along, no such sight to be shown,
But to rejoice in splendour of mine own.

Exeunt

Act 1, Scene 3

A room in Capulet's house

Enter LADY CAPULET and NURSE

LADY CAPULET
Thou knowest my daughter's of a pretty age.

NURSE
On Lammas eve at night shall she be fourteen.
I remember it well. 'Tis since the earthquake
Now eleven years; and she was wean'd,
I never shall forget it.

Enter JULIET

Thou wast the prettiest babe that e'er I nursed:
An I might live to see thee married once,
I have my wish.

LADY CAPULET
That 'marry' is the very theme
I came to talk of. Tell me daughter Juliet,
How stands your disposition to be married?

JULIET
It is an honour that I dream not of.

LADY CAPULET
Well, think of marriage now, younger than you
Here in Verona, ladies of esteem,
Are made already mothers; thus then in brief:
The valiant Paris seeks you for his love.

NURSE
Why, he's a man of wax, young lady.

LADY CAPULET
This night you shall behold him at our feast,
Read o'er the volume of young Paris' face,
And find delight writ there with beauty's pen:
Can you love the gentleman?

JULIET
I'll look to like, if looking liking move:
But no more deep will I endart mine eye,
Than your consent gives strength to make it fly.

Exeunt

Act 1, Scene 4

A street

Enter ROMEO, MERCUTIO and BENVOLIO

ROMEO
Give me a torch, I am not for this ambling.

MERCUTIO
You are a lover; borrow Cupid's wings,
And soar with them above a common bound.

ROMEO
I am too sore enpierced with his shaft,
To soar with his light feathers.

MERCUTIO
And to sink in it should you burden love,
Too great oppression for a tender thing.
In delay we waste our lights in vain, like lamps by day.

ROMEO
And we mean well in going to this mask;
But 'tis no wit to go.

MERCUTIO
Why may one ask?

ROMEO
I dream'd a dream tonight.

MERCUTIO
And so did I.

ROMEO
Well what was yours?

MERCUTIO
That dreamers often lie.

ROMEO
In bed asleep, while they do dream things true.

CHORUS
O, then, we see Queen Mab hath been with you:
She is the fairies' midwife, and she comes
In shape no bigger than an agate-stone
On the fore-finger of an alderman,
Drawn with a team of little atomies
Athwart men's noses as they lie asleep:
Her wagon-spokes made of long spinners' legs,
The cover of the wings of grasshoppers,
Her traces of the smallest spider's web,
Her collars of the moonshine's watery beams,
Her whip of cricket's bone, the lash of film,
Her wagoner a small grey-coated gnat,
Not half so big as a round little worm
Prick'd from the lazy finger of a maid;
Her chariot is an empty hazel-nut
Made by the joiner squirrel or old grub,
Time out o'mind the fairies' coachmakers.
And in this state she gallops night by night
Through lovers' brains: and then they dream of love;
O'er courtiers' knees, that dream on curtsies straight,
O'er lawyers' fingers, who straight dream on fees,
O'er ladies' lips, who straight on kisses dream,
Which oft the angry Mab with blisters plagues,
Because their breaths with sweetmeats tainted are.
Sometime she gallops o'er a courtier's nose,
And then dreams he of smelling out a suit;

And sometime comes she with a tithe-pig's tail
Tickling a parson's nose as a'lies asleep,
Then he dreams of another benefice:
Sometime she driveth o'er a soldier's neck,
And then dreams he of cutting foreign throats,
Of breaches, ambuscadoes, Spanish blades,
Of healths five fathom deep,
And then anon drums in his ear,
At which he starts and wakes,
And being thus frighted swears a prayer or two
And sleeps again.

ROMEO
Thou talk'st of nothing.

MERCUTIO
True, they talk of dreams,
Which are the children of an idle brain,
Begot of nothing, but vain fantasy.

BENVOLIO
Supper is done, and we shall come too late.

ROMEO
I fear too early, for my mind misgives,
Some consequence yet hanging in the stars,
Shall bitterly begin his fearful date
With this night's revels, and expire the term
Of a despised life clos'd in my breast:
By some vile forfeit of untimely death.
But He, that hath the steerage of my course,
Direct my sail: on lusty gentlemen.

Exeunt

Act 1, Scene 5

A hall in Capulet's house

Musical interlude. Enter CAPULET, LADY CAPULET, TYBALT and JULIET

CAPULET
[Addressing audience]
Welcome, gentlemen,
Ladies that have their toes
Unplagued with corns, will walk about with you:
Ah my mistresses, which of you
Will now deny to dance?
You are welcome, gentlemen, come musicians play.
Give room, and foot it girls.

Enter ROMEO

ROMEO
O, she doth teach the torches to burn bright:
Did my heart love till now? Forswear it, sight,
For I ne'er saw true beauty till this night.

TYBALT
This by his voice, should be a Montague.
To strike him dead, I hold it not a sin.
[To CAPULET] Uncle, this is
A villain that is hither come in spite,
To scorn at our solemnity this night.

CAPULET
Content thee gentle coz, let him alone,
He bears him like a portly gentleman:

And to say truth, Verona brags of him,
To be a virtuous and well govern'd youth:
Therefore be patient, take no note of him.

TYBALT
Why uncle, 'tis a shame.

CAPULET
You are a saucy boy:
You are a princox, go,
Be quiet, or I'll make you quiet.

TYBALT
I will withdraw, but this intrusion shall
Now seeming sweet convert to bitter gall.

Exeunt TYBALT, CAPULET and LADY CAPULET

ROMEO
If I profane with my unworthiest hand,
This holy shrine, the gentle sin is this,
My lips, two blushing pilgrims did ready stand
To smooth that rough touch, with a tender kiss.

JULIET
Good pilgrim,
You do wrong your hand too much.
Which mannerly devotion shows in this,
For saints have hands, that pilgrims' hands do touch,
And palm to palm, is holy palmers' kiss.

ROMEO
Have not saints lips, and holy palmers too?

JULIET
Ay, pilgrim, lips that they must use in prayer.

ROMEO
O, then, dear saint, let lips do what hands do.

JULIET
Saints do not move,
Though grant for prayers' sake.

ROMEO
Then move not while my prayer's effect I take:
Thus from my lips, by thine my sin is purged.

JULIET
You kiss by th'book.

Enter NURSE

NURSE
Madam your mother craves a word with you.

ROMEO
What is her mother?

NURSE
Her mother is the lady of the house.

ROMEO
Is she a Capulet?
O dear account! My life is my foe's debt.

Exit

JULIET
Come hither nurse,
What is yond gentleman that follows there?

NURSE
His name is Romeo, and a Montague.

JULIET
My only love sprung from my only hate,
Too early seen, unknown, and known too late.

NURSE
Anon, anon:
Come, let's away, the strangers all are gone.

Exeunt

CHORUS
Now old desire doth in his death bed lie,
And young affection gapes to be his heir,
That fair, for which love groan'd for and would die,
With tender Juliet match'd, is now not fair.
Now Romeo is beloved, and loves again,
Alike bewitched by the charm of looks:
But to his foe supposed he must complain,
And she steal love's sweet bait from fearful hooks:
Being held a foe, he may not have access
To breathe such vows as lovers use to swear,
And she as much in love, her means much less,
To meet her new beloved any where:
But passion lends them power, time, means to meet,
Tempering extremities with extreme sweet.

ACT 2, SCENE 1

THE CAPULET ORCHARD

Enter ROMEO

ROMEO
He jests at scars that never felt a wound.

JULIET appears above

But soft, what light through yonder window breaks?
It is the east, and Juliet is the sun.
It is my lady, O it is my love.
She speaks yet she says nothing:
See how she leans her cheek upon her hand.
O that I were a glove upon that hand.

JULIET
Ay me.

ROMEO
O speak again bright angel.

JULIET
O Romeo, Romeo, wherefore art thou Romeo?
Deny thy father and refuse thy name:
Or if thou wilt not, be but sworn my love,
And I'll no longer be a Capulet.
What's in a name? That which we call a rose
By any other name would smell as sweet.

ROMEO
Call me but love, and I'll be new baptized,
Henceforth I never will be Romeo.

JULIET
What man art thou, that thus bescreen'd in night
So stumblest on my counsel?

ROMEO
My name dear saint, is hateful to myself,
Because it is an enemy to thee.

JULIET
Art thou not Romeo, and a Montague?

ROMEO
Neither fair maid, if either thee dislike.

JULIET
O gentle Romeo,
If thou dost love, pronounce it faithfully.

ROMEO
Lady, by yonder moon I vow,
That tips with silver all these fruit-tree tops.

JULIET
O swear not by the moon, th'inconstant moon,
Lest that thy love prove likewise variable.

ROMEO
What shall I swear by?

JULIET
Do not swear at all:
Or, if thou wilt, swear by thy gracious self,
Which is the god of my idolatry.
Although I joy in thee,
I have no joy of this contract tonight,
It is too rash, too unadvis'd, too sudden,
Too like the lightning. Sweet, good night.

ROMEO
O wilt thou leave me so unsatisfied?

JULIET
What satisfaction canst thou have tonight?

ROMEO
Th'exchange of thy love's faithful vow for mine.

JULIET
I gave thee mine before thou didst request it:
And yet I would it were to give again.

NURSE calls within

I hear some noise within; dear love, adieu.
If that thy bent of love be honourable,
Thy purpose marriage, send me word tomorrow,
Where and what time thou wilt perform the rite.

NURSE
[Within] Madam!

JULIET
(By and by, I come.)
A thousand times good night!

Exit, above

ROMEO
A thousand times the worse, to want thy light.

Re-enter JULIET, above

39

JULIET
Romeo, at what o'clock tomorrow
Shall I send to thee?

ROMEO
By the hour of nine.

JULIET
I will not fail: 'tis twenty years till then.
Good night.

ROMEO
Parting is such sweet sorrow,
That I shall say good night till it be morrow.

JULIET
Sleep dwell upon thine eyes, peace in thy breast.

Exit

ROMEO
Would I were sleep and peace, so sweet to rest.

Exit

Act 2, Scene 2

Friar Laurence's cell

Enter FRIAR LAURENCE

FRIAR LAURENCE
I must up-fill this osier cage of ours,
With baleful weeds, and precious juiced flowers,
The earth that's nature's mother, is her tomb;
What is her burying grave that is her womb:
And from her womb children of divers kind
We sucking on her natural bosom find,
Many for many virtues excellent:
None but for some and yet all different.

Enter ROMEO

ROMEO
Good morrow father.

FRIAR LAURENCE
What early tongue so sweet saluteth me?
Thy earliness doth me assure
Thou art uprous'd by some distemperature;
Or if not so, our Romeo hath not been in bed tonight.

ROMEO
That last is true.

FRIAR LAURENCE
God pardon sin: wast thou with Rosaline?

ROMEO
With Rosaline, my ghostly father? No,
I have forgot that name, and that name's woe.
I have been feasting with mine enemy,
Where on a sudden one hath wounded me,
That's by me wounded. My heart's dear love is set
On the fair daughter of rich Capulet:
As mine on hers, so hers is set on mine;
And all combin'd, save what thou must combine
By holy marriage: this I pray,
That thou consent to marry us today.

FRIAR LAURENCE
What a change is here! Young men's love then lies
Not truly in their hearts, but in their eyes.
In one respect, I'll thy assistant be:
For this alliance may so happy prove,
To turn your households' rancour to pure love.

ROMEO
O let us hence; I stand on sudden haste.

FRIAR LAURENCE
Wisely and slow, they stumble that run fast.

Exeunt

ACT 2, SCENE 3

A STREET

Enter BENVOLIO and MERCUTIO

BENVOLIO
Tybalt hath sent a letter to Montague's house.

MERCUTIO
A challenge on my life.

BENVOLIO
Romeo will answer it.

MERCUTIO
Alas poor Romeo, he is already dead; run through the ear
With a love-song; and is he a man to encounter Tybalt?

Enter NURSE

NURSE
God ye good morrow gentlemen.

MERCUTIO
God ye good den fair gentlewoman.

Enter ROMEO

NURSE
[To ROMEO] Sir, I desire some confidence with you.

MERCUTIO
A bawd, a bawd, a bawd.
Romeo, will you come to your father's?
We'll to dinner thither.

ROMEO
I will follow you.

Exeunt MERCUTIO and BENVOLIO

NURSE
My young lady bade me inquire you out.

ROMEO
Nurse, commend me to thy lady and mistress.
Bid her devise some means to come to shrift this afternoon,
And there she shall at Friar Laurence' cell
Be shriv'd and married.

NURSE
This afternoon sir? Well she shall be there.
O, there is a nobleman in town, one Paris,
That would fain lay knife aboard;
I anger her sometimes, and tell her that Paris
Is the properer man; but when I say so, she looks
As pale as any clout in the versal world.

ROMEO
Commend me to thy lady.

NURSE
Ay a thousand times.

Exeunt

Act 2, Scene 4

The Capulet Orchard

Enter JULIET

JULIET
In half an hour she promised to return.
From nine till twelve is three long hours,
Yet my nurse is not come.

Enter NURSE

O honey nurse what news?

NURSE
I am a-weary, give me leave awhile.

JULIET
Nay come I pray thee speak.

NURSE
Do you not see that I am out of breath?

JULIET
How art thou out of breath, when thou hast breath
To say to me that thou art out of breath?
Is thy news good, or bad?
What says he of our marriage? What of that?

NURSE
O, my back, my back.

JULIET
Sweet, sweet, sweet nurse, tell me, what says my love?

NURSE
Your love says like an honest gentleman,
And a courteous, and a kind, and a handsome,
And I warrant a virtuous: where is your mother?

JULIET
Where is my mother?
Why, she is within;
Come, what says Romeo?

NURSE
Have you got leave to go to shrift today?

JULIET
I have.

NURSE
Then hie you hence to Friar Laurence' cell,
There stays a husband to make you a wife:
Go, I'll to dinner, hie you to the cell.

JULIET
Hie to high fortune, honest nurse, farewell.

Exeunt

ACT 2, SCENE 5

FRIAR LAURENCE'S CELL

Enter FRIAR LAURENCE and ROMEO

ROMEO
Do thou but close our hands with holy words,
Then love-devouring death do what he dare,
It is enough. I may but call her mine.

FRIAR LAURENCE
These violent delights have violent ends
And in their triumph: die like fire and powder;
Which as they kiss consume. The sweetest honey
Is loathsome in his own deliciousness,
And in the taste confounds the appetite.
Therefore love moderately, long love doth so,
Too swift arrives as tardy as too slow.
Here comes the lady.

Enter JULIET

ROMEO
Ah Juliet, if the measure of thy joy
Be heap'd like mine, and that thy skill be more
To blazon it, then sweeten with thy breath
This neighbour air, and let rich music's tongue
Unfold the imagin'd happiness that both
Receive in either, by this dear encounter.

JULIET
Conceit more rich in matter than in words,
Brags of his substance, not of ornament:
They are but beggars that can count their worth,
But my true love is grown to such excess,
I cannot sum up some of half my wealth.

FRIAR LAURENCE
Come, come with me, and we will make short work,
For by your leaves, you shall not stay alone,
Till holy church incorporate two in one.

Exeunt

ACT 3, SCENE 1

A PUBLIC PLACE

Enter MERCUTIO and BENVOLIO

BENVOLIO
I pray thee good Mercutio let's retire,
The day is hot, the Capulets abroad:
And if we meet, we shall not scape a brawl.

MERCUTIO
Why, thou hast quarrelled with a man for coughing in the street,
Because he hath wakened thy dog that hath lain asleep in the sun:
And yet thou wilt tutor me from quarrelling?

BENVOLIO
By my head, here come the Capulets.

Enter TYBALT

TYBALT
Gentlemen, good den, a word with one of you.

MERCUTIO
And but one word with one of us? Couple it with
Something, make it a word and a blow.

BENVOLIO
Either withdraw unto some private place,
And reason coldly of your grievances:
Or else depart, here all eyes gaze on us.

MERCUTIO
I will not budge for no man's pleasure, I.

Enter ROMEO

TYBALT
Well, peace be with you sir, here comes my man.
Romeo, the hate I bear thee can afford
No better term than this: thou art a villain.

ROMEO
Tybalt, the reason that I have to love thee,
Doth much excuse the appertaining rage
To such a greeting: therefore farewell.

TYBALT
Boy, this shall not excuse the injuries
That thou hast done me; therefore turn and draw.

ROMEO
I do protest I never injur'd thee,
But love thee better than thou canst devise.

MERCUTIO
O calm, dishonourable, vile submission:
Tybalt, you rat-catcher, will you walk?

Draws

TYBALT
I am for you.

They fight

ROMEO
Tybalt, Mercutio, the prince expressly hath
Forbidden bandying in Verona streets.

TYBALT stabs MERCUTIO under ROMEO's arm, and flees

MERCUTIO
I am hurt. A scratch, a scratch;
'Tis not so deep as a well, nor so wide as a
Church door; but 'tis enough, 'twill serve.
A plague o'both your houses.
Help me into some house, Benvolio,
They have made worms' meat of me.

Exeunt MERCUTIO and BENVOLIO

ROMEO
My very friend hath got his mortal hurt
In my behalf, my reputation stain'd
With Tybalt's slander, Tybalt that an hour
Hath been my cousin: O sweet Juliet,
Thy beauty hath soften'd valour's steel.

Re-enter BENVOLIO and TYBALT

BENVOLIO
O Romeo, Romeo, brave Mercutio's dead;
Here comes the furious Tybalt back again.

ROMEO
Fire and fury be my conduct now.
Now Tybalt take the villain back again
That late thou gav'st me, for Mercutio's soul
Is but a little way above our heads,
Staying for thine to keep him company:
Either thou or I, or both, must go with him.

TYBALT
Thou wretched boy shalt with him hence.

They fight. TYBALT dies

BENVOLIO
Romeo, away be gone:
Stand not amaz'd, the prince will doom thee death.

ROMEO
O! I am fortune's fool.

***Exit ROMEO. Enter PRINCE, MONTAGUE, LADY
MONTAGUE, CAPULET and LADY CAPULET***

PRINCE
Where are the vile beginners of this fray?

BENVOLIO
There lies the man, slain by young Romeo,
That slew thy kinsman brave Mercutio.

LADY CAPULET
O prince, O cousin, husband, O, the blood is spilt
Of my dear kinsman. Prince as thou art true,
For blood of ours, shed blood of Montague.

PRINCE
Who began this bloody fray?

CHORUS
Tybalt, here slain, whom Romeo's hand did slay,
Romeo that spoke him fair,
Bid him bethink how nice the quarrel was,
And urg'd withal your high displeasure:
All this uttered with gentle breath,
Calm look, knees humbly bow'd
Could not take truce with the unruly spleen
Of Tybalt deaf to peace,
But that he tilts with piercing steel
At bold Mercutio's breast,

Who all as hot, turns deadly point to point,
And with a martial scorn,
With one hand beats cold death aside,
And with the other sends it back to Tybalt,
Whose dexterity retorts it:
Romeo he cries aloud,
'Hold, friends, friends part,'
And swifter than his tongue,
His agile arm beats down their fatal points,
And 'twixt them rushes, underneath whose arm,
An envious thrust from Tybalt,
Hit the life of stout Mercutio,
And then Tybalt fled.
But by and by comes back to Romeo,
Who had but newly entertained revenge,
And to't they go like lightning,
Was stout Tybalt slain.
And as he fell, did Romeo turn and fly.

LADY CAPULET
Romeo slew Tybalt, Romeo must not live.

PRINCE
Romeo slew him, he slew Mercutio,
Who now the price of his dear blood doth owe?

MONTAGUE
Not Romeo, prince, he was Mercutio's friend,
His fault concludes, but what the law should end,
The life of Tybalt.

PRINCE
And for that offence,
Immediately we do exile him hence:
I will be deaf to pleading and excuses,
Nor tears, nor prayers shall purchase out abuses.
Therefore use none, let Romeo hence in haste,
Else when he is found, that hour is his last.

Exeunt

Act 3, Scene 2

The Capulet house

CHORUS
Gallop apace, you fiery-footed steeds,
And bring in cloudy night immediately.
Spread thy close curtain love-performing night,
That run-away's eyes may wink, and Romeo
Leap to Juliet's arms, untalk'd of and unseen.
Come civil night, thou sober-suited matron,
Come night, come Romeo, come thou day in night,
For thou wilt lie upon the wings of night
Whiter than new snow on a raven's back:
Come gentle night, come loving blackbrow'd night.
Give Juliet her Romeo, and when he shall die,
Take him and cut him out in little stars,
And he will make the face of heaven so fine,
That all the world will be in love with night,
And pay no worship to the garish sun.
So tedious is this day, as is the night before some festival
To an impatient child that hath new robes
And may not wear them.

Enter JULIET and NURSE

JULIET
What news?
Why dost thou wring thy hands?

NURSE
Ah, well-a-day, he's dead, he's dead
O Romeo, Romeo,
Who ever would have thought it?

JULIET
What devil art thou,
That dost torment me thus?
Hath Romeo slain himself?

NURSE
O Tybalt, Tybalt, the best friend I had:
That ever I should live to see thee dead.

JULIET
What storm is this that blows so contrary?
Is Romeo slaughter'd? And is Tybalt dead?

NURSE
Tybalt is gone, and Romeo that kill'd him is banished.

JULIET
O God!
Did Romeo's hand shed Tybalt's blood?
O serpent heart, hid with a flowering face.
O that deceit should dwell
In such a gorgeous palace.

NURSE
There's no trust, no faith, no honesty in men,
Shame come to Romeo.

JULIET
Blister'd be thy tongue
For such a wish, he was not born to shame:
O what a beast was I to chide at him.

NURSE
Will you speak well of him
That kill'd your cousin?

JULIET
Shall I speak ill of him that is my husband?
Back, foolish tears, back to your native spring.
My husband lives that Tybalt would have slain,
And Tybalt's dead that would have slain my husband:
All this is comfort; wherefore weep I then?
'Tybalt is dead, and Romeo banished;'
To speak that word is father, mother,
Tybalt, Romeo, Juliet, all slain, all dead.

Exeunt

Act 3, Scene 3

Friar Laurence's cell

Enter FRIAR LAURENCE and ROMEO

ROMEO
Father, what news?
What less than dooms day
Is the prince's doom?

FRIAR LAURENCE
Not body's death, but body's banishment.

ROMEO
Ha, banishment? Be merciful, say 'death:'
There is no world without Verona walls,
But purgatory, torture, hell itself.

FRIAR LAURENCE
O rude unthankfulness!
This is dear mercy, and thou seest it not.

ROMEO
'Tis torture, and not mercy: heaven is here,
Where Juliet lives.
And say'st thou yet that exile is not death?

FRIAR LAURENCE
I'll give thee armour to keep off that word,
Adversity's sweet milk, philosophy.

ROMEO
Hang up philosophy:
Unless philosophy can make a Juliet,
Displant a town, reverse a prince's doom.
Wert thou as young as I, Juliet thy love,
An hour but married, Tybalt murdered,
Doting like me, and like me banished,
Then mightst thou speak,
Then mightst thou tear thy hair,
And fall upon the ground as I do now.

FRIAR LAURENCE
The law that threaten'd death became thy friend
And turn'd it to exile, there art thou happy.
Go get thee to thy love as was decreed,
Ascend her chamber, hence and comfort her:
But look thou stay not till the watch be set,
For then thou canst not pass to Mantua;
Where thou shalt live till we can find a time
To blaze your marriage, reconcile your friends,
Beg pardon of thy prince, and call thee back.

ROMEO
How well my comfort is reviv'd by this.

FRIAR LAURENCE
Go hence,
Good night;
Be gone before the watch be set:
Sojourn in Mantua, I'll find out your man,
And he shall signify from time to time,
Every good hap to you, that chances here:
Give me thy hand, 'tis late, farewell, good night.

Exeunt

ACT 3, SCENE 4

A ROOM IN CAPULET'S HOUSE

Enter CAPULET, LADY CAPULET and PARIS

CAPULET
Sir Paris, I will make a desperate tender
Of my child's love: I think she will be rul'd
In all respects by me. Wife, go you to her;
Acquaint her here of my son Paris' love;
A Thursday tell her,
She shall be married to this noble earl.
Farewell my lord, light to my chamber, ho.
Afore me, it is so late, that we may call it early by and by,
Goodnight.

Exeunt

Act 3, Scene 5

The Capulet orchard

Enter ROMEO and JULIET above

JULIET
Wilt thou be gone? It is not yet near day:
Yond light is not daylight: therefore stay yet,
Thou need'st not to be gone.

ROMEO
Let me be ta'en, let me be put to death;
I have more care to stay, than will to go:
Come death and welcome.
Let's talk, it is not day.

JULIET
It is, it is, hie hence, be gone away:
It is the lark that sings so out of tune,
Straining harsh discords, and unpleasing sharps.
O now be gone, more light and light it grows.

ROMEO
More light and light, more dark and dark our woes.

ROMEO descends

JULIET
I must hear from thee every day in the hour,
For in a minute there are many days.

ROMEO
Farewell:
I will omit no opportunity,
That may convey my greetings love, to thee.

JULIET
O God! I have an ill-divining soul,
Methinks I see thee, now thou art so low,
As one dead in the bottom of a tomb,
Either my eyesight fails, or thou look'st pale.

ROMEO
And trust me love, in my eye so do you:
Dry sorrow drinks our blood. Adieu, adieu.

Exit

LADY CAPULET
[Within] Ho daughter, are you up?

JULIET
Who is't that calls? Is it my lady mother?

Enter LADY CAPULET

LADY CAPULET
Why how now Juliet?
I'll tell thee joyful tidings girl.
Marry my child, early next Thursday morn,
The County Paris at Saint Peter's Church,
Shall happily make thee a joyful bride.

JULIET
He shall not make me there a joyful bride.
I pray you tell my lord and father madam,
I will not marry yet, and when I do, I swear
It shall be Romeo, whom you know I hate
Rather than Paris.

Enter CAPULET and NURSE

CAPULET
Have you delivered to her our decree?

LADY CAPULET
Ay, sir;
But she will none.
I would the fool were married to her grave.

CAPULET
How now? Will she none? Doth she not give us thanks?
Doth she not count her blest, that we have wrought
So worthy a gentleman to be her bridegroom?
Fettle your fine joints 'gainst Thursday next,
To go with Paris to Saint Peter's Church:
Or I will drag thee on a hurdle thither.

JULIET
Good father, I beseech you on my knees
Hear me with patience, but to speak a word.

CAPULET
I tell thee what, get thee to church a Thursday,
Or never after look me in the face.
Day, night, hour, tide, time, work, play,
Alone, in company, still my care hath been
To have her match'd:
And then to have a wretched puling fool,
To answer 'I'll not wed; I cannot love,
I am too young; I pray you, pardon me.'
But, as you will not wed, I'll pardon you:
Graze where you will, you shall not house with me.

Exit

JULIET
O, sweet my mother, cast me not away,
Delay this marriage for a month, a week.

LADY CAPULET
Talk not to me: do as thou wilt,
For I have done with thee.

Exit

JULIET
O nurse, how shall this be prevented?

NURSE
Romeo is banished;
Since the case so stands as now it doth,
I think it best you married with the county.
I think you are happy in this second match,
For it excels your first: or if it did not,
Your first is dead, or 'twere as good he were.

JULIET
Speakest thou from thy heart?

NURSE
And from my soul too.

JULIET
Well, thou hast comforted me marvellous much.
Go in, and tell my lady I am gone,
Having displeas'd my father, to Laurence' cell,
To make confession, and to be absolv'd.

NURSE
Marry I will, and this is wisely done.

Exit

JULIET
I'll to the friar to know his remedy,
If all else fail, myself have power to die.

Exit

ACT 4, SCENE 1

FRIAR LAURENCE'S CELL

Enter FRIAR LAURENCE and JULIET

JULIET
Are you at leisure, holy father now?
I must and nothing may prorogue it,
On Thursday next be married to the county.
Tell me how I may prevent it:
Give me some present counsel, or behold
'Twixt my extremes and me, this bloody knife
Shall play the umpire, arbitrating that,
Which the commission of thy years and art,
Could to no issue of true honour bring.

FRIAR LAURENCE
Hold daughter: if, rather than to marry County Paris,
Thou hast the strength of will to slay thyself,
Then is it likely thou wilt undertake
A thing like death to chide away this shame,
And if thou dar'st, I'll give thee remedy.
Go home, be merry, give consent
To marry Paris: Wednesday is tomorrow,
Tomorrow night look that thou lie alone;
Take thou this vial being then in bed,
And this distilling liquor drink thou off,
When presently through all thy veins shall run,
A cold and drowsy humour: for no pulse
Shall keep his native progress, but surcease:
No warmth, no breath shall testify thou livest,
The roses in thy lips and cheeks shall fade
To many ashes, the eyes' windows fall

Like death when he shut up the day of life:
And in this borrowed likeness of shrunk death
Thou shalt continue two and forty hours,
And then awake as from a pleasant sleep.
Now when the bridegroom in the morning comes,
To rouse thee from thy bed, there art thou dead:
Then in thy best robes uncover'd on the bier
Thou shalt be borne to that same ancient vault
Where all the kindred of the Capulets lie,
In the mean time against thou shalt awake,
Shall Romeo by my letters know our drift,
And hither shall he come, and that very night
Shall Romeo bear thee hence to Mantua.
I'll send a friar with speed
To Mantua with my letters to thy lord.

JULIET
Love give me strength,
And strength shall help afford.
Farewell dear father.

Exeunt

ACT 4, SCENE 2

JULIET'S CHAMBER

Enter CAPULET and NURSE

CAPULET
What is my daughter gone to Friar Laurence?

NURSE
Well he may chance to do some good on her.

Enter JULIET

CAPULET
How now my headstrong,
Where have you been gadding?

JULIET
Where I have learnt me to repent the sin
Of disobedient opposition: I am enjoin'd
By holy Laurence to fall prostrate here,
And beg your pardon: pardon I beseech you.

CAPULET
Why, I am glad on't, this is well, stand up,
I will walk myself to County Paris, to prepare him up
Against tomorrow, my heart is wondrous light,
Since this same wayward girl is so reclaim'd.

Exit CAPULET

JULIET
Gentle nurse, I pray thee, leave me to my self tonight:
For I have need of many orisons.

Exit NURSE

Farewell:
God knows when we shall meet again.
I have a faint cold fear thrills through my veins,
That almost freezes up the heat of fire:
Come, vial, what if this mixture do not work at all?
Shall I be married then tomorrow morning?
No, no, this shall forbid it. Lie thou there.

Laying down a dagger

What if it be a poison which the friar
Subtly hath minister'd to have me dead,
Lest in this marriage he should be dishonour'd,
Because he married me before to Romeo?
How, if when I am laid into the tomb,
I wake before the time that Romeo
Come to redeem me?
Shall I not, then, be stifled in the vault,
To whose foul mouth no healthsome air breathes in,
And there die strangled ere my Romeo comes?
O if I wake, shall I not be distraught,
And madly play with my forefathers' joints?
And pluck the mangled Tybalt from his shroud?
And in this rage with some great kinsman's bone,
(As with a club) dash out my desperate brains?
O look, methinks I see my cousin's ghost,
Seeking out Romeo that did spit his body
Upon a rapier's point: stay Tybalt, stay;
Romeo, Romeo, Romeo, here's drink: I drink to thee.

JULIET falls upon her bed

ACT 4, SCENE 3

JULIET'S CHAMBER

CAPULET
[Within] Come, stir, stir, stir,
The second cock hath crow'd,
Go waken Juliet, go and trim her up;
I'll go and chat with Paris:
Make haste, the bridegroom he is come already.

Enter NURSE

NURSE
Mistress, what mistress? Juliet?
What not a word? How sound is she asleep.
What, dress'd, and in your clothes?
Alas, alas, help, help, my lady's dead.

Enter LADY CAPULET

LADY CAPULET
What noise is here?

NURSE
Look, look, O heavy day.

LADY CAPULET
O me, O me, my child, my only life:
Revive, look up, or I will die with thee.

Enter CAPULET

NURSE
She's dead: deceased, she's dead: alack the day.

CAPULET
Ha? Let me see her: out alas she's cold,
Her blood is settled and her joints are stiff.

Enter FRIAR LAURENCE and PARIS

FRIAR LAURENCE
Come, is the bride ready to go to church?

CAPULET
Ready to go, but never to return.

NURSE
Most lamentable day, most woeful day,
That ever, ever, I did yet behold.

PARIS
O love, O life, not life, but love in death.

FRIAR LAURENCE
Dry up your tears, and stick your rosemary
On this fair corse, and as the custom is,
In her best array bear her to church.

CAPULET
All things that we ordained festival,
Turn from their office to black funeral.

FRIAR LAURENCE
Sir go you in; every one prepare
To follow this fair corse unto her grave:
The heavens do lour upon you, for some ill:
Move them no more, by crossing their high will.

Exeunt

Act 5, Scene 1

A street in Mantua

Enter ROMEO

ROMEO
I dreamt my lady came and found me dead,
And breath'd such life with kisses in my lips,
That I revived.

Enter BALTHASAR

How now Balthasar? How fares my Juliet?
For nothing can be ill, if she be well.

BALTHASAR
Then she is well, and nothing can be ill.
Her body sleeps in Capel's monument,
And her immortal part with angels lives.

ROMEO
Is it even so?
Then I defy you stars.
Get me ink and paper, and hire post-horses;
I will hence tonight.
Hast thou no letters to me from the friar?

BALTHASAR
No my good lord.

Exit BALTHASAR

ROMEO
Well Juliet, I will lie with thee tonight:
I do remember an apothecary,
And hereabouts he dwells, which late I noted
In tatter'd weeds, meagre were his looks,
Noting this penury, to myself I said
'An if a man did need a poison now,
Whose sale is present death in Mantua,
Here lives a caitiff wretch would sell it him.'

Enter APOTHECARY

What ho? Apothecary?
Hold, there is forty ducats: let me have
A dram of poison, such soon speeding gear,
As will disperse itself through all the veins,
That the life-weary-taker may fall dead.

APOTHECARY
Such mortal drugs I have, but Mantua's law
Is death to any he, that utters them.

ROMEO
Need and oppression starveth in thy eyes,
The world is not thy friend, nor the world's law.

APOTHECARY
My poverty, but not my will consents.

ROMEO
There's thy gold,
Get thyself in flesh.
Come cordial, and not poison, go with me
To Juliet's grave, for there must I use thee.

Exeunt

Act 5, Scene 2

Friar Laurence's cell

Enter FRIAR JOHN and FRIAR LAURENCE

FRIAR LAURENCE
Welcome from Mantua, what says Romeo?

FRIAR JOHN
Going to find a bare-foot brother out,
One of our order to associate me,
Here in this city visiting the sick,
And finding him, the searchers of the town
Suspecting that we both were in a house
Where the infectious pestilence did reign,
Seal'd up the doors, and would not let us forth,
So that my speed to Mantua there was stay'd.

FRIAR LAURENCE
Who bare my letter then to Romeo?

FRIAR JOHN
I could not send it, here it is again,
Nor get a messenger to bring it thee,
So fearful were they of infection.

FRIAR LAURENCE
The letter was not nice, but full of charge,
Of dear import, and the neglecting it
May do much danger:
Now must I to the monument alone,
Within three hours will fair Juliet wake,
I will write again to Mantua,
And keep her at my cell till Romeo come.

Exeunt

ACT 5, SCENE 3

A CHURCHYARD IN VERONA AND THE CAPULET VAULT WITHIN IT

Enter PARIS

PARIS
Sweet flower with flowers thy bridal bed I strew.

Retires. Enter ROMEO and BALTHASAR

ROMEO
Hold take this letter, early in the morning
See thou deliver it to my lord and father.
Hence, be gone.

BALTHASAR
I will be gone sir, and not trouble you.

ROMEO
Farewell good fellow.

Exit BALTHASAR

Thou detestable maw, thou womb of death,
Gorg'd with the dearest morsel of the earth:
Thus I enforce thy rotten jaws to open,
And in despite, I'll cram thee with more food.

Opens the tomb. Enter PARIS

PARIS
This is that banish'd haughty Montague,
That murder'd my love's cousin: I will apprehend him.
Condemned villain, I do apprehend thee.

ROMEO
Good gentle youth, tempt not a desperate man,
Put not another sin upon my head,
By urging me to fury.

PARIS
I do apprehend thee for a felon here.

ROMEO
Wilt thou provoke me? Then have at thee boy.

They fight

PARIS
O I am slain.

Dies

ROMEO
O my love, my wife,
Death that hath suck'd the honey of thy breath,
Hath had no power yet upon thy beauty:
Thou art not conquer'd; beauty's ensign yet
Is crimson in thy lips, and in thy cheeks,
And death's pale flag is not advanced there.
Ah dear Juliet: why art thou yet so fair?
Shall I believe, that unsubstantial death is amorous,
And that the lean abhorred monster keeps
Thee here in dark to be his paramour?
O here will I set up my everlasting rest,
And shake the yoke of inauspicious stars
From this world-wearied flesh.
Come bitter conduct, come, unsavoury guide,
Thou desperate pilot, now at once run on
The dashing rocks thy sea-sick weary bark:
Here's to my love.

Drinks

O true apothecary!
Thy drugs are quick. Thus with a kiss I die.

Dies. Enter FRIAR LAURENCE

FRIAR LAURENCE
Romeo, oh pale: who else? What Paris too?
And steep'd in blood? Ah what an unkind hour
Is guilty of this lamentable chance?
The lady stirs.

JULIET wakes

JULIET
O comfortable friar, where's my lord?

Noise within

FRIAR LAURENCE
I hear some noise lady. Come, come away.
Thy husband in thy bosom there lies dead:
And Paris too. Come I'll dispose of thee
Among a sisterhood of holy nuns:
Stay not to question, for the watch is coming.
Come, go good Juliet.
I dare no longer stay.

Exit FRIAR LAURENCE

JULIET
Go get thee hence, for I will not away,
What's here? A cup clos'd in my true love's hand?
Poison I see hath been his timeless end:
O churl, drunk all? And left no friendly drop
To help me after, I will kiss thy lips,
Haply some poison yet doth hang on them,
To make die with a restorative.

Kisses him. Noise within

Thy lips are warm.
Yea, noise?
Then I'll be brief. O happy dagger.

Snatching ROMEO's dagger

This is thy sheath.

Stabs herself

There rust and let me die.

Falls on ROMEO's body, and dies. Enter the PRINCE,
FRIAR LAURENCE, BALTHASAR, CAPULET and LADY
CAPULET

PRINCE
What misadventure is so early up,
That calls our person from our morning's rest?

CAPULET
The people in the street cry Romeo.
Some Juliet, and some Paris, and all run,
With open outcry toward our monument.

PRINCE
Here lies the County Paris slain,
And Romeo dead, and Juliet dead before,
Warm and new kill'd.
Here is a friar, and slaughter'd Romeo's man,
With instruments upon them fit to open
These dead men's tombs.

CAPULET
O heaven!
O wife look how our daughter bleeds!

LADY CAPULET
O me, this sight of death, is as a bell,
That warns my old age to a sepulchre.

Enter MONTAGUE

PRINCE
Come Montague, for thou art early up,
To see thy son and heir, now early down.

MONTAGUE
O thou untaught, what manners is in this,
To press before thy father to a grave?

PRINCE
Seal up the mouth of outrage for a while,
Till we can clear these ambiguities,
And then I will be general of your woes:
Meantime forbear and let mischance be slave to patience.
Say at once what thou dost know in this.

CHORUS
Romeo there dead, was husband to that Juliet,
And she there dead, that's Romeo's faithful wife:
Their stol'n marriage day was Tybalt's dooms day,
Whose untimely death
Banish'd the new-made bridegroom from this city:
For whom (and not for Tybalt) Juliet pined.
She was betroth'd and would have been married
To County Paris: then comes she to the friar,
And (with wild looks) bid him devise some means
To rid her from this second marriage,
Or in his cell there would she kill herself.
Then he gave her, a sleeping potion;
Which so took effect and wrought on her
The form of death: meantime he writ to Romeo,
That he should hither come, as this dire night,
To help to take her from her borrowed grave,
Being the time the potion's force should cease.
But he which bore the letter, Friar John,
Was stay'd by accident; and yesternight
Return'd the letter back. Then all alone,
At the prefixed hour of her waking,
Came the friar to take her from her kindred's vault,
Meaning to keep her closely at his cell,
Till he conveniently could send to Romeo.
But when he came (some minute ere the time
Of her awaking) here untimely lay
The noble Paris, and true Romeo dead.
She wakes, and he entreated her come forth,
And bear this work of heaven, with patience:
But then, a noise did scare him from the tomb,
And she (too desperate) would not go with him,
But (as it seems) did violence on herself.

PRINCE
See, what a scourge is laid upon your hate,
That heaven finds means to kill your joys with love;
And I, for winking at your discords too,
Have lost a brace of kinsmen: all are punish'd.

CAPULET
O brother Montague, give me thy hand,
This is my daughter's jointure, for no more
Can I demand.

MONTAGUE
I will raise her statue in pure gold,
That while Verona by that name is known,
There shall no figure at such rate be set
As that of true and faithful Juliet.

CAPULET
As rich shall Romeo by his lady lie,
Poor sacrifices of our enmity.

Exeunt

EPILOGUE

CHORUS
A glooming peace this morning with it brings,
The sun for sorrow will not show his head;
Go hence, to have more talk of these sad things,
Some shall be pardon'd, and some punished.
For never was a story of more woe,
Than this of Juliet, and her Romeo.

MACBETH

INTRODUCTION

Evil, ambition, betrayal, and the supernatural all combine in this extremely dark tragedy. Condensing Shakespeare's original play into an hour only serves to intensify the horror as Macbeth, fortified by Lady Macbeth, wades further and further into his bloody mess. The original play, famously, has three witches. As the Chorus provides the witches' lines in this adaptation, there is flexibility as to the quantity of these 'weird sisters'. While there are far fewer lines than in Shakespeare's original, the core soliloquies have been retained to ensure that the workings of Macbeth's mind are still conveyed to the audience. The final battle – the real battle between Macbeth and Malcolm was at Lumphanan in 1057 – still takes place, though Birnam Wood moves to Dunsinane at a swiftness to which most audiences will be unaccustomed.

Synopsis

There has been a rebellion against the Scottish king, Duncan; Macbeth and Banquo have excelled in putting down that rebellion. One of the rebels, the Thane of Cawdor, is to be executed for his disloyalty; Macbeth is to take on the honour and title in his stead. Macbeth and Banquo are travelling through a heath when they encounter 'weird sisters' or witches – in this version played by the Chorus. The witches prophesy that Macbeth shall be Thane of Cawdor and then king, while Banquo will produce a line of kings, though he will not be king himself. The prophecy appears to be coming true when news reaches Macbeth that from henceforth he will, indeed, be Thane of Cawdor. However, an obstacle to Macbeth's further promotion appears when Duncan bestows the title of Prince of Cumberland on his heir and son, Malcolm.

Macbeth writes to his wife about his encounter with the witches and their prophecy. Lady Macbeth fears that Macbeth does not have the mental strength to ensure that all of the prophecy comes true. Duncan is to stay at Macbeth's castle that night; Lady Macbeth resolves to play her part in his stay and, we surmise, his death. Macbeth has second thoughts about murdering Duncan, but Lady Macbeth persuades him to go ahead. Macbeth is to stab Duncan, then leave the daggers on the king's guards, implicating them in the murder. (Macbeth stabs the guards, and later claims it was revenge for their murder of Duncan.) The plan goes ahead, but Macbeth is perturbed and returns to Lady Macbeth with the daggers. Lady Macbeth undertakes to return the daggers to the guards. Duncan's body is discovered. The king's sons, Malcolm and Donalbain, flee – the former to England, the latter to Ireland – though this only serves to cast suspicion on them for orchestrating their father's death. Macbeth and Lady Macbeth are invested as king and queen at Scone.

Banquo grows suspicious of Macbeth, as the witches' prophecy has, so far, come true. But the witches have also prophesied that Banquo will beget a line of kings, so Macbeth arranges for him to be murdered. Macbeth also plans to have Banquo's son, Fleance, murdered, but Fleance flees. Macbeth hosts a feast, at which the ghost of Banquo appears. Macbeth has a fit when he sees the ghost; Lady Macbeth insists that the lords assembled for the feast leave. Macbeth returns to the witches to find out more about their prophecy. He encounters a series of apparitions, the first of which warns him to 'beware Macduff'. The second tells him that 'none of woman born shall harm Macbeth'. The third warns Macbeth that he will be vanquished when Birnam Wood moves to Dunsinane. The ghost of Banquo reappears, following an apparition of a train of eight kings.

Macbeth is informed that Macduff has fled to England. Macbeth arranges for Macduff's wife and children to be murdered. News reaches Macduff about his family's demise; Malcolm encourages Macduff to get revenge against Macbeth. Meanwhile, a doctor and a gentlewoman observe Lady Macbeth in a kind of trance, trying to clean the spots off her hands – hands previously bedaubed with Duncan's blood.

Troops rally near Dunsinane to overthrow Macbeth. Macbeth himself muses on the warnings given him by the apparitions. Malcolm tells his troops each to cut down a bough from Birnam Wood, and to carry it ahead of them to disguise their progress towards Macbeth's castle. Macbeth hears a cry, which is Lady Macbeth killing herself. He is then informed that Birnam Wood is indeed moving towards Dunsinane. Macduff enters. As one 'from his mother's womb untimely ripp'd', Macduff is the man not 'of woman born' whom Macbeth should fear. Macbeth and Macduff fight. As Macbeth's other enemies advance on his castle, Macduff reappears with Macbeth's head. Malcolm will now be King of Scotland.

CAST

(in order of appearance)

Chorus of witches and apparitions
Duncan
Malcolm
Donalbain
Lennox
Ross
Macbeth
Banquo
Angus
Lady Macbeth
Macduff
First Murderer
Second Murderer
Fleance
Three apparitions
Lady Macduff
Macduff's son
Doctor
Gentlewoman
Menteith
Caithness
Seyton
Siward

PROLOGUE

Thunder

CHORUS
When shall we all meet again?
In thunder, lightning, or in rain?
When the hurly-burly's done,
When the battle's lost, and won.
That will be ere the set of sun.
Where the place?
Upon the heath.
There to meet with Macbeth.
I come, Graymalkin.
Paddock calls anon.
Fair is foul, and foul is fair:
Hover through the fog and filthy air.

ACT 1, SCENE 1

A CAMP NEAR FORRES

Alarum. Enter DUNCAN, MALCOLM, DONALBAIN and LENNOX

DUNCAN
Donalbain, my son, can report,
The newest state of the revolt.

MALCOLM
Hail, brother! Say to the king, our father,
The knowledge of the broil
As thou didst leave it.

DONALBAIN
Your Majesty, doubtful it stood;
The merciless Macdonwald
From the Western Isles of Kerns and Gallowglasses
Is supplied: but all's too weak:
For brave Macbeth disdaining fortune,
With his brandish'd steel carv'd out his passage,
Till he faced the slave:
Which ne'er shook hands, nor bad farewell to him,
Till he unseam'd him from the nave to th'chaps,
And fix'd his head upon our battlements.
No sooner justice had with valour arm'd,
Compell'd these skipping kerns to trust their heels,
But the Norweyan lord surveying vantage,
With furbish'd arms and new supplies of men,
Began a fresh assault.

DUNCAN
Dismay'd not this our captains,
Macbeth and Banquo?

DONALBAIN
Yes; I must report they were
As cannons over-charg'd with double cracks,
So they doubly redoubled strokes upon the foe.

DUNCAN
So well thy words smack of honour.
Who comes here?

Enter ROSS

MALCOLM
The worthy Thane of Ross.

LENNOX
What a haste looks through his eyes?
So should he look, that seems to speak things strange.

ROSS
I come from Fife, great king,
Where the Norweyan banners flout the sky.
Norway himself, assisted by that most disloyal traitor
The Thane of Cawdor, began a dismal conflict,
Till that Bellona's bridegroom, lapp'd in proof,
Confronted him with self-comparisons,
Point against point, rebellious arm 'gainst arm.
Curbing his lavish spirit: and, to conclude,
The victory fell on us.

DUNCAN
Great happiness.
No more that Thane of Cawdor shall deceive
Our bosom interest: go pronounce his present death,
And with his former title greet Macbeth.
What he hath lost, noble Macbeth hath won.

Exeunt

Act 1, Scene 2

A heath near Forres

CHORUS
Where hast thou been?
Killing swine.
Where thou?
A sailor's wife had chestnuts in her lap,
And munch'd, and munch'd, and munch'd:
'Give me,' quoth I:
'Aroint thee, witch!' the rump-fed ronyon cries.
Her husband's to Aleppo gone, master o' the Tiger:
But in a sieve I'll thither sail,
And like a rat without a tail,
I'll do, I'll do, and I'll do.
I'll give thee a wind.
Thou'rt kind.
And I another.
I myself have all the other,
And the very ports they blow,
All the quarters that they know
I'th'shipman's card.
I will drain him dry as hay:
Sleep shall neither night nor day
Hang upon his pent-house lid:
He shall live a man forbid:
Weary se'nnights, nine times nine,
Shall he dwindle, peak and pine:
Though his bark cannot be lost,
Yet it shall be tempest-tost.
Look what I have.
Show me, show me.
Here I have a pilot's thumb,
Wreck'd as homeward he did come.

Drum

A drum, a drum:
Macbeth doth come.
The weird sisters, hand in hand,
Posters of the sea and land,
Thus do go, about, about:
Thrice to thine, and thrice to mine,
And thrice again, to make up nine.
Peace, the charm's wound up.

Enter MACBETH and BANQUO

MACBETH
What are these, so wither'd, and so wild in their attire,
That look not like the inhabitants o'th'earth?
Speak, if you can: what are you?

CHORUS
All hail Macbeth, hail to thee, Thane of Glamis.
All hail Macbeth, hail to thee, Thane of Cawdor.
All hail Macbeth, that shalt be king hereafter.

BANQUO
My noble partner you greet with present grace,
And great prediction of noble having, and of royal hope,
That he seems rapt withal: to me you speak not.
If you can look into the seeds of time,
And say which grain will grow, and which will not,
Speak then to me.

CHORUS
Hail.
Hail.
Hail.
Lesser than Macbeth, and greater.

Not so happy, yet much happier.
Thou shalt get kings, though thou be none:
So all hail, Macbeth and Banquo.
Banquo, and Macbeth, all hail.

MACBETH
Stay, you imperfect speakers, tell me more:
I know I am Thane of Glamis, but how of Cawdor?
The Thane of Cawdor lives: and to be king
Stands not within the prospect of belief,
No more than to be Cawdor.

BANQUO
Have we eaten on the insane root,
That takes the reason prisoner?

MACBETH
Your children shall be kings.

BANQUO
You shall be king.

MACBETH
And Thane of Cawdor too: went it not so?

Enter ROSS and ANGUS

ROSS
The king hath happily receiv'd, Macbeth,
The news of thy success: and when he reads
Thy personal venture in the rebels' fight,
His wonders and his praises do contend,
Which should be thine, or his:
He bad me, from him, call thee Thane of Cawdor.

BANQUO
What, can the devil speak true?

MACBETH
The Thane of Cawdor lives.

ANGUS
But under heavy judgment bears that life,
Which he deserves to lose.
Whether he was combined with those of Norway,
Or did line the rebel with hidden help
And vantage, I know not:
But treasons capital, confess'd, and prov'd,
Have overthrown him.

MACBETH
[Aside] Glamis, and Thane of Cawdor:
The greatest is behind.

To BANQUO

Do you not hope your children shall be kings,
When those that gave the Thane of Cawdor to me,
Promised no less to them?

BANQUO
That trusted home,
Might yet enkindle you unto the crown,
Besides the Thane of Cawdor. But 'tis strange:
And oftentimes, to win us to our harm,
The instruments of darkness tell us truths,
Win us with honest trifles, to betray's
In deepest consequence.

Exit

MACBETH
Two truths are told,
As happy prologues to the swelling act
Of the imperial theme. This supernatural soliciting
Cannot be ill, cannot be good:
If ill, why hath it given me earnest of success,
Commencing in a truth? I am Thane of Cawdor.
If good, why do I yield to that suggestion,
Whose horrid image doth unfix my hair,
And make my seated heart knock at my ribs?
Present fears are less than horrible imaginings:
My thought, whose murder yet is but fantastical,
Shakes so my single state of man,
That function is smother'd in surmise,
And nothing is but what is not.
If chance will have me king,
Why, chance may crown me,
Without my stir.
Come what come may,
Time, and the hour, runs through the roughest day.

Exit

ACT 1, SCENE 3

THE PALACE AT FORRES

***Flourish. Enter DUNCAN, MALCOLM, DONALBAIN and
LENNOX***

DUNCAN
Is execution done on Cawdor?

MALCOLM
I have spoke with one that saw him die:
Who did report, that he confess'd his treasons,
Implor'd your highness' pardon and set forth
A deep repentance.

Enter MACBETH, BANQUO, ROSS and ANGUS

DUNCAN
O worthiest cousin,
The sin of my ingratitude even now
Was heavy on me. Thou art so far before,
That swiftest wing of recompense is slow,
To overtake thee. Would thou hadst less deserv'd,
That the proportion both of thanks, and payment,
Might have been mine: only I have left to say,
More is thy due, than more than all can pay.

MACBETH
The service, and the loyalty I owe,
In doing it, pays itself.
Your highness' part, is to receive our duties:
And our duties are to your throne, and state,
Children and servants.

DUNCAN
I have begun to plant thee, and will labour
To make thee full of growing. Noble Banquo,
That hast no less deserv'd, nor must be known
No less to have done so.

BANQUO
There if I grow,
The harvest is your own.

DUNCAN
Sons, kinsmen, thanes, know
We will establish our estate upon
Our eldest, Malcolm, whom we name hereafter,
The Prince of Cumberland: which honour must
Not unaccompanied invest him only,
But signs of nobleness, like stars, shall shine
On all deservers. From hence to Inverness,
And bind us further to you.

MACBETH
The rest is labour, which is not us'd for you:
I'll be myself the harbinger and make joyful
The hearing of my wife, with your approach.

Flourish. Exeunt all but MACBETH

The Prince of Cumberland: that is a step,
On which I must fall down, or else o'erleap,
For in my way it lies. Stars hide your fires,
Let not light see my black and deep desires:
The eye wink at the hand: yet let that be,
Which the eye fears, when it is done to see.

Exit

Act 2, Scene 1

Macbeth's castle at Inverness

Enter LADY MACBETH reading a letter

LADY MACBETH
"They met me in the day of success: and I have
learn'd they have more in them, than mortal knowledge.
Whiles I stood rapt in the wonder of it,
Came missives from the king, who all-hailed me
Thane of Cawdor, by which title before,
These weird sisters saluted me, and referr'd
Me to the coming on of time, with 'Hail, king that
Shalt be!' This have I thought good to deliver
Thee (my dearest partner of greatness) that thou
Mightst not lose the dues of rejoicing by being
Ignorant of what greatness is promised thee."
Glamis thou art, and Cawdor, and shalt be
What thou art promis'd: yet do I fear thy nature,
It is too full o'th'milk of human kindness,
To catch the nearest way. Thou wouldst be great,
Art not without ambition, but without
The illness should attend it. What thou wouldst highly,
That wouldst thou holily: wouldst not play false,
And yet wouldst wrongly win. Hie thee hither,
That I may pour my spirits in thine ear,
And chastise with the valour of my tongue
All that impedes thee from the golden round.
The king comes here tonight.
The raven himself is hoarse
That croaks the fatal entrance of Duncan
Under my battlements. Come you spirits,
That tend on mortal thoughts: make thick my blood,
Stop up the access and passage to remorse.

Enter MACBETH

Great Glamis, worthy Cawdor.

MACBETH
Greater than both, by the all-hail hereafter.

LADY MACBETH
Your face, my thane, is as a book where men
May read strange matters. To beguile the time,
Look like the time; look like the innocent flower,
But be the serpent under't.

MACBETH
He that's coming, must be provided for.

LADY MACBETH
You shall put this night's business into my dispatch,
Which shall to all our nights, and days to come,
Give solely sovereign sway, and masterdom.

***Exit MACBETH. Enter DUNCAN, MALCOLM,
DONALBAIN, BANQUO, LENNOX, MACDUFF, ROSS and
ANGUS***

DUNCAN
See, see our honour'd hostess.

LADY MACBETH
All our service, in every point twice done
And then done double, were poor, and single business,
To contend against those honours, deep, and broad,
Wherewith your majesty loads our house.

DUNCAN
Where's the thane of Cawdor?
We coursed him at the heels, and had a purpose
To be his purveyor: but he rides well,
And his great love (sharp as his spur) hath holp him
To his home before us.
Conduct me to mine host, we love him highly,
And shall continue our graces towards him.

Exeunt

ACT 2, SCENE 2

THE SAME

Enter MACBETH

MACBETH
If it were done, when 'tis done, then 'twere well
It were done quickly: if th'assassination
Could trammel up the consequence, and catch
With his surcease, success: that but this blow
Might be the be all, and the end all. Here,
But here, upon this bank and shoal of time,
We'ld jump the life to come. But in these cases,
We still have judgment here, that we but teach
Bloody instructions, which being taught, return
To plague th'inventor, this even-handed justice
Commends th'ingredients of our poison'd chalice
To our own lips. He's here in double trust;
First, as I am his kinsman, and his subject,
Strong both against the deed: then, as his host,
Who should against his murderer shut the door,
Not bear the knife myself. Besides, this Duncan
Hath borne his faculties so meek; hath been
So clear in his great office, that his virtues
Will plead like angels, trumpet-tongu'd against
The deep damnation of his taking-off:
And pity, like a naked new-born-babe,
Striding the blast, or heaven's cherubim, hors'd
Upon the sightless couriers of the air,
Shall blow the horrid deed in every eye,
That tears shall drown the wind. I have no spur
To prick the sides of my intent, but only
Vaulting ambition, which o'erleaps itself
And falls on th'other.

Enter *LADY MACBETH*

LADY MACBETH
He has almost supp'd: why have you left the chamber?

MACBETH
We will proceed no further in this business.

LADY MACBETH
Was the hope drunk, wherein you dress'd yourself?
Hath it slept since? And wakes it now,
To look so green and pale at what it did so freely?
Art thou afeard to be the same in thine own act,
And valour, as thou art in desire?
What made you break this enterprise to me?
When you durst do it, then you were a man:
And, to be more than what you were, you would
Be so much more the man.

MACBETH
If we should fail?

LADY MACBETH
We fail?
But screw your courage to the sticking-place,
And we'll not fail: when Duncan is asleep,
His two chamberlains
Will I with wine, and wassail, so convince,
That memory shall be a fume,
And the receipt of reason
A limbeck only: when in swinish sleep,
Their drenched natures lie as in a death,
What cannot you and I perform upon
Th'unguarded Duncan? What not put upon
His spongy officers, who shall bear the guilt
Of our great quell?

MACBETH
Will it not be receiv'd,
When we have mark'd with blood those sleepy two
Of his own chamber, and used their very daggers,
That they have done't?

LADY MACBETH
Who dares receive it other,
As we shall make our griefs and clamour roar
Upon his death?

MACBETH
I am settled.
Away, and mock the time with fairest show,
False face must hide what the false heart doth know.

Exit LADY MACBETH

MACBETH
Is this a dagger, which I see before me,
The handle toward my hand? Come, let me clutch thee:
I have thee not, and yet I see thee still.
Art thou not, fatal vision, sensible
To feeling, as to sight? Or art thou but
A dagger of the mind, a false creation,
Proceeding from the heat-oppressed brain?
I see thee yet, in form as palpable
As this which now I draw.
Thou marshall'st me the way that I was going,
And such an instrument I was to use.
Mine eyes are made the fools o'th'other senses,
Or else worth all the rest: I see thee still;
And on thy blade, and dudgeon, gouts of blood,
Which was not so before. There's no such thing:
It is the bloody business, which informs
Thus to mine eyes. Now o'er the one half world

Nature seems dead, and wicked dreams abuse
The curtain'd sleep: witchcraft celebrates
Pale Hecate's offerings: and wither'd murder,
Alarum'd by his sentinel, the wolf,
Whose howl's his watch, thus with his stealthy pace.
With Tarquin's ravishing strides, towards his design
Moves like a ghost. Whiles I threat, he lives:
Words to the heat of deeds too cold breath gives.

Bell

I go, and it is done: the bell invites me.
Hear it not, Duncan, for it is a knell,
That summons thee to heaven, or to hell.

Exit

ACT 2, SCENE 3

THE SAME

Enter LADY MACBETH

LADY MACBETH
That which hath made them drunk hath made me bold:
What hath quench'd them, hath given me fire.
He is about it, the doors are open: and the grooms
Do mock their charge with snores.
Alack, I am afraid they have awak'd,
And 'tis not done. Th'attempt, and not the deed,
Confounds us. I laid their daggers ready,
He could not miss 'em. Had he not resembled
My father as he slept, I had done't.

Enter MACBETH

MACBETH
I have done the deed:
There's one did laugh in's sleep, and one cried 'Murder!',
That they did wake each other: I stood, and heard them:
But they did say their prayers, and address'd them again to sleep.
One cried 'God bless us', and 'Amen' the other.
As they had seen me with these hangman's hands:
Methought I heard a voice cry
'Glamis hath murder'd sleep, and therefore Cawdor
Shall sleep no more; Macbeth shall sleep no more.'

LADY MACBETH
You do unbend your noble strength, to think
So brain-sickly of things: go get some water,
And wash this filthy witness from your hand.
Why did you bring these daggers from the place?

They must lie there: go carry them, and smear
The sleepy grooms with blood.

MACBETH
I'll go no more:
I am afraid, to think what I have done.

LADY MACBETH
Infirm of purpose:
Give me the daggers: if he do bleed,
I'll gild the faces of the grooms withal,
For it must seem their guilt.

Knocking

MACBETH
Whence is that knocking?
How is't with me, when every noise appals me?
What hands are here? Ha: they pluck out mine eyes.
Will all great Neptune's ocean wash this blood
Clean from my hand?

Knocking

LADY MACBETH
Be not lost so poorly in your thoughts.
I hear a knocking at the south entry:
Retire I to our chamber.

Exit LADY MACBETH. Enter MACDUFF and LENNOX

MACDUFF
Our knocking has awak'd him.
Is the king stirring, worthy thane?

MACBETH
Not yet.

MACDUFF
He did command me to call timely on him.

MACBETH
I'll bring you to him.

MACDUFF
I know this is a joyful trouble to you:
But yet 'tis one.

MACBETH
The labour we delight in, physics pain.

MACDUFF
I'll make so bold to call,
For 'tis my limited service.

Exit MACDUFF

LENNOX
Goes the king hence today?

MACBETH
He did appoint so.

LENNOX
The night has been unruly: where we lay,
Our chimneys were blown down.

MACBETH
'Twas a rough night.

Re-enter MACDUFF

MACDUFF
O horror, horror, horror,
Tongue nor heart cannot conceive, nor name thee.
Most sacrilegious murder hath broke ope
The Lord's anointed temple, and stole thence
The life o'th'building.
Approach the chamber, see,
And then speak yourselves.

Exeunt MACBETH and LENNOX

Awake, awake,
Ring the alarum bell. Murder and treason,
Banquo, and Donalbain, Malcolm awake,
Up, up, and see the great doom's image:
Malcolm, Banquo, as from your graves rise up,
And walk like sprites, to countenance this horror.

Enter BANQUO and LADY MACBETH

O Banquo, Banquo,
Our royal master's murder'd.

BANQUO
I prithee, contradict thyself,
And say, it is not so.

LADY MACBETH
Woe, alas. What, in our house?

Re-enter MACBETH and LENNOX, with ROSS

MACBETH
Had I but died an hour before this chance,
I had lived a blessed time: for from this instant,
There's nothing serious in mortality:
All is but toys: renown and grace is dead.

Enter MALCOLM and DONALBAIN

DONALBAIN
What is amiss?

MACDUFF
Your royal father's murder'd.

MALCOLM
By whom?

LENNOX
Those of his chamber, as it seem'd, had done't:
Their hands and faces were badged with blood,
So were their daggers, which we found upon their pillows.

MACBETH
O, yet I do repent me of my fury,
That I did kill them.

MACDUFF
Wherefore did you so?

MACBETH
Who can be wise, amaz'd, temperate, and furious,
Loyal, and neutral, in a moment? Here lay Duncan,
His silver skin laced with his golden blood:
There the murderers, steep'd in the colours of their trade;
Their daggers unmannerly breech'd with gore.

LADY MACBETH
Help me hence, ho.

MACDUFF
Look to the lady.

*LADY MACBETH is carried out. Exeunt all but MALCOLM
and DONALBAIN*

MALCOLM
What will you do?
Let's not consort with them:
To show an unfelt sorrow, is an office
Which the false man does easy.
I'll to England.

DONALBAIN
To Ireland, I:
Our separated fortune shall keep us both the safer:
Where we are, there's daggers in men's smiles:
The near in blood, the nearer bloody.

MALCOLM
This murderous shaft that's shot
Hath not yet lighted: and our safest way,
Is to avoid the aim. Therefore, to horse,
And let us not be dainty of leave-taking,
But shift away: there's warrant in that theft,
Which steals itself, when there's no mercy left.

Exeunt

Act 2, Scene 4

Outside Macbeth's castle

Enter ROSS and MACDUFF

ROSS
Is't known who did this more than bloody deed?

MACDUFF
Those that Macbeth hath slain were suborn'd:
Malcolm and Donalbain, the king's two sons,
Are stol'n away and fled, which puts upon them
Suspicion of the deed.

ROSS
'Gainst nature still,
Thriftless ambition, that will raven up
Thine own life's means: then 'tis most like,
The sovereignty will fall upon Macbeth.

MACDUFF
He is already nam'd, and gone to Scone
To be invested.

ROSS
Will you to Scone?

MACDUFF
No cousin, I'll to Fife.

ROSS
Well, I will thither.

MACDUFF
Well, may you see things well done there: adieu
Lest our old robes sit easier than our new.

Exeunt

Act 3, Scene 1

The palace at Forres

Enter BANQUO

BANQUO
Thou hast it now, king, Cawdor, Glamis, all,
As the weird women promis'd, and I fear,
Thou play'dst most foully for't: yet it was said
It should not stand in thy posterity,
But that myself should be the root, and father
Of many kings. But hush, no more.

Enter MACBETH as king

MACBETH
We hear, our bloody cousins are bestow'd
In England and in Ireland, not confessing
Their cruel parricide.
Tonight we hold a solemn supper sir,
And I'll request your presence.

BANQUO
Let your highness command upon me,
To the which my duties are with
A most indissoluble tie for ever knit.

MACBETH
Ride you this afternoon?

BANQUO
Ay, my good lord.

MACBETH
Is't far you ride?

BANQUO
As far as will fill up the time
'Twixt this and supper.

MACBETH
Fail not our feast.

BANQUO
My lord, I will not.

MACBETH
Hie you to horse: adieu, till you return at night.
Goes Fleance with you?

BANQUO
Ay, my good lord.

MACBETH
I wish your horses swift and sure of foot.

Exit BANQUO

Our fears in Banquo stick deep,
And in his royalty of nature reigns that
Which would be fear'd. 'Tis much he dares,
And to that dauntless temper of his mind,
He hath a wisdom, that doth guide his valour,
To act in safety. There is none but he,
Whose being I do fear; he chid the sisters
When first they put the name of king upon me,
And bad them speak to him. Then prophet-like,
They hail'd him father to a line of kings.
If't be so, for Banquo's issue have I filed my mind,

For them the gracious Duncan have I murder'd,
Put rancours in the vessel of my peace
Only for them; to make the seed of Banquo kings.
Rather than so, come fate into the list,
And champion me to the utterance!
Who's there?

Enter TWO MURDERERS

FIRST MURDERER
I am one, my liege,
Whom the vile blows and buffets of the world
Have so incens'd, that I am reckless what I do,
To spite the world.

SECOND MURDERER
And I another,
So weary with disasters, tugg'd with fortune,
That I would set my life on any chance,
To mend it, or be rid on't.

MACBETH
Banquo is your enemy, so is he mine:
And in such bloody distance,
That every minute of his being, thrusts
Against my near'st of life.

FIRST MURDERER
We shall, my lord,
Perform what you command us.

MACBETH
Your spirits shine through you.
It must be done tonight, and something from the palace:
And with him leave no rubs nor botches in the work:
Fleance his son, that keeps him company,

Too must embrace the fate of that dark hour.
It is concluded. Banquo, thy soul's flight,
If it find heaven, must find it out tonight.

Exeunt

Act 3, Scene 2

The Same

Enter LADY MACBETH

LADY MACBETH
Nought's had, all's spent,
Where our desire is got without content:
'Tis safer, to be that which we destroy,
Than by destruction dwell in doubtful joy.

Enter MACBETH

How now, my lord, why do you keep alone,
Of sorriest fancies your companions making,
Using those thoughts, which should indeed have died
With them they think on? What's done is done.
Be bright and jovial among your guests tonight.

MACBETH
So shall I love, and so I pray be you:
Let your remembrance apply to Banquo,
Present him eminence, both with eye and tongue:
Unsafe the while, that we must make
Our faces vizards to our hearts,
Disguising what they are.
Thou know'st, that Banquo and his Fleance lives.

LADY MACBETH
What's to be done?

MACBETH
Be innocent of the knowledge,
Till thou applaud the deed: come, seeling night,

Scarf up the tender eye of pitiful day,
And with thy bloody and invisible hand
Cancel and tear to pieces that great bond
Which keeps me pale.
Good things of day begin to droop, and drowse,
While night's black agents to their preys do rouse.

Exeunt

Act 3, Scene 3

A park near the palace

Enter MURDERERS

FIRST MURDERER
The west yet glimmers with some streaks of day.

SECOND MURDERER
Hark, I hear horses.

BANQUO
[Within] Give us a light there, ho.

SECOND MURDERER
'Tis he:
The rest already are i'th'court.

FIRST MURDERER
His horses go about.

SECOND MURDERER
Almost a mile: but he does usually,
So all men do, from hence to th'palace gate
Make it their walk.

Enter BANQUO and FLEANCE

FIRST MURDERER
'Tis he.

SECOND MURDERER
Stand to't.

FLEANCE
It will be rain tonight.

FIRST MURDERER
Let it come down.

They set upon BANQUO

BANQUO
O, treachery! Fly, good Fleance, fly, fly, fly,
Thou may'st revenge. O slave!

Dies. FLEANCE escapes

SECOND MURDERER
There's but one down: the son is fled.

FIRST MURDERER
Well, let's away, and say how much is done.

Exeunt

Act 3, Scene 4

A hall in the palace

Enter MACBETH, LADY MACBETH, ROSS and LENNOX

MACBETH
You know your own degrees, sit down:
Ourself will mingle with society,
And play the humble host.

LADY MACBETH
Pronounce it for me, sir, to all our friends,
For my heart speaks they are welcome.

FIRST MURDERER stands at the door

MACBETH
See, they encounter thee with their hearts' thanks.
Anon we'll drink a measure the table round.

Approaches the door

There's blood upon thy face.

FIRST MURDERER
'Tis Banquo's then.

MACBETH
Is he dispatch'd?

FIRST MURDERER
Ay, my good lord: safe in a ditch he bides.
Yet most royal sir, Fleance is scap'd.

MACBETH
I am cabin'd, cribb'd, confin'd, bound in
To saucy doubts and fears. The worm that's fled
Hath nature that in time will venom breed.
Get thee gone.

Exit FIRST MURDERER

LENNOX
May't please your highness sit.

GHOST OF BANQUO enters, and sits in MACBETH's place

MACBETH
Here had we now our country's honour roof'd,
Were the grac'd person of our Banquo present:
Who may I rather challenge for unkindness
Than pity for mischance.

ROSS
His absence (sir) lays blame upon his promise.
Please't your highness to grace us with your royal company?

MACBETH
The table's full.

LENNOX
Here is a place reserv'd, sir.

MACBETH
Where?

LENNOX
Here, my good lord.
What is't that moves your highness?

MACBETH
Thou canst not say I did it: never shake
Thy gory locks at me.

ROSS
Gentlemen, rise: his highness is not well.

LADY MACBETH
Pray you, keep seat; the fit is momentary;
[To MACBETH] Are you a man?
O, these flaws and starts, would well become
A woman's story at a winter's fire,
Shame itself. Why do you make such faces?

MACBETH
Prithee, see there: how say you?
Why, what care I? If thou canst nod, speak too.

Exit GHOST OF BANQUO

The times have been, that when the brains were out,
The man would die: but now they rise again
With twenty mortal murders on their crowns.

LADY MACBETH
My worthy lord,
Your noble friends do lack you.

MACBETH
I do forget:
My most worthy friends,
I have a strange infirmity, which is nothing
To those that know me.
Come, love and health to all: give me some wine.

Re-enter GHOST OF BANQUO

MACBETH
Avaunt, quit my sight, thy blood is cold.
Hence, horrible shadow,
Unreal mock'ry, hence.

Exit GHOST OF BANQUO

LADY MACBETH
[To MACBETH] You have displaced the mirth,
With most admired disorder.
[To LENNOX] He grows worse and worse;
At once, good night: stand not upon the order of your going,
But go at once.

LENNOX
Good night, and better health
Attend his majesty.

LADY MACBETH
A kind good night to all.

Exeunt all but MACBETH and LADY MACBETH

MACBETH
I will tomorrow to the weird sisters.
More shall they speak; for now I am bent to know
By the worst means, the worst.
I am in blood stepp'd in so far that, should I wade no more,
Returning were as tedious as go o'er:
Strange things I have in head, that will to hand,
Which must be acted, ere they may be scann'd.

Exeunt

Act 4, Scene 1

A heath near Forres

Thunder

CHORUS
Thrice the brinded cat hath mew'd.
Thrice and once the hedge-pig whin'd.
Harpier cries 'tis time, 'tis time.
Round about the cauldron go:
In the poison'd entrails throw.
Toad, that under cold stone
Days and nights has thirty one:
Swelter'd venom sleeping got,
Boil thou first i'th'charmed pot.
Double, double toil and trouble;
Fire burn, and cauldron bubble.
Fillet of a fenny snake,
In the cauldron boil and bake:
Eye of newt, and toe of frog,
Wool of bat, and tongue of dog,
Adder's fork and blind-worm's sting,
Lizard's leg, and owlet's wing,
For a charm of powerful trouble,
Like a hell-broth, boil and bubble.
Double, double toil and trouble,
Fire burn and cauldron bubble.
Scale of dragon, tooth of wolf,
Witches' mummy, maw and gulf
Of the ravin'd salt-sea shark:
Root of hemlock, digg'd i'th'dark,
Finger of birth-strangled babe
Ditch-deliver'd by a drab,

Make the gruel thick and slab:
Add thereto a tiger's chaudron,
For the ingredients of our cauldron.
Double, double toil and trouble,
Fire burn, and cauldron bubble.
Cool it with a baboon's blood,
Then the charm is firm and good.
And now about the cauldron sing,
Like elves and fairies in a ring,
Enchanting all that you put in.
By the pricking of my thumbs,
Something wicked this way comes.
Open, locks,
Whoever knocks!

Enter MACBETH

MACBETH
How now, you secret, black, and midnight hags?
What is't you do?

CHORUS
A deed without a name.

MACBETH
I conjure you, answer me to what I ask you.

CHORUS
Speak.
Demand.
We'll answer.
Say, if thou'dst rather hear it from our mouths,
Or from our masters?

MACBETH
Call 'em; let me see 'em.

CHORUS
Pour in sow's blood, that hath eaten
Her nine farrow: grease that's sweaten
From the murderer's gibbet throw
Into the flame. Come, high or low;
Thyself and office deftly show.

Thunder. First apparition appears: an armed head

MACBETH
Tell me, thou unknown power.

CHORUS
He knows thy thought:
Hear his speech, but say thou nought.

FIRST APPARITION
Macbeth, Macbeth, Macbeth, beware Macduff,
Beware the thane of Fife. Dismiss me. Enough.

Descends

MACBETH
Whate'er thou art, for thy good caution, thanks;
Thou hast harp'd my fear aright: but one
Word more.

CHORUS
He will not be commanded: here's another,
More potent than the first.

Thunder. Second apparition appears: a bloody child

SECOND APPARITION
Macbeth, Macbeth, Macbeth,
Be bloody, bold, and resolute; laugh to scorn

The power of man, for none of woman born
Shall harm Macbeth.

Descends

MACBETH
Then live, Macduff: what need I fear of thee?
But yet I'll make assurance double sure,
And take a bond of fate: thou shalt not live;
That I may tell pale-hearted fear it lies,
And sleep in spite of thunder.

***Thunder. Third apparition appears: a child crowned with a
tree in his hand***

What is this that rises like the issue of a king,
And wears upon his baby-brow, the round
And top of sovereignty?

CHORUS
Listen, but speak not to't.

THIRD APPARITION
Macbeth shall never vanquish'd be, until
Great Birnam wood to high Dunsinane hill
Shall come against him.

Descends

MACBETH
That will never be: who can impress the forest,
Bid the tree unfix his earth-bound root?
Yet my heart throbs to know one thing:
Tell me, if your art can tell so much:
Shall Banquo's issue ever reign in this kingdom?

CHORUS
Seek to know no more.

MACBETH
Deny me this and an eternal curse fall on you:
Let me know. What noise is this?

Hautboys

CHORUS
Show.
Show.
Show.
Show his eyes, and grieve his heart;
Come like shadows, so depart.

**Eight kings appear, the last with a glass in his hand; GHOST
OF BANQUO follows**

MACBETH
Thou art too like the spirit of Banquo: down:
Thy crown does sear mine eyeballs.
Why do you show me this?
What, will the line stretch out to the crack of doom?
Another yet. I'll see no more:
And yet the eighth appears, who bears a glass
Which shows me many more.
Horrible sight. Now, I see, 'tis true;
For the blood-bolter'd Banquo smiles upon me,
And points at them for his.

Apparitions vanish. Enter LENNOX

LENNOX
My lord, Macduff is fled to England.

MACBETH
From this moment, the very firstlings of my heart
Shall be the firstlings of my hand.
The castle of Macduff, I will surprise,
Give to the edge o'the sword his wife,
His babes, and all unfortunate souls
That trace him in his line. No boasting like a fool,
This deed I'll do, before this purpose cool.

Exeunt

Act 4, Scene 2

Macduff's castle at Fife

Enter LADY MACDUFF, her SON and ROSS

LADY MACDUFF
What had he done, to make him fly the land?

ROSS
You must have patience madam.

LADY MACDUFF
He had none:
His flight was madness: when our actions do not,
Our fears do make us traitors.

ROSS
You know not whether it was his wisdom, or his fear.
I take my leave of you:
Shall not be long but I'll be here again:
Things at the worst will cease, or else climb upward
To what they were before.

Exit

LADY MACDUFF
Wisdom? To leave his wife, to leave his babes,
His mansion and his titles in a place
From whence himself does fly?

Enter MURDERERS

What are these faces?

FIRST MURDERER
Where is your husband?

LADY MACDUFF
I hope, in no place so unsanctified
Where such as thou mayst find him.

SECOND MURDERER
He's a traitor.

SON
Thou liest, thou shag-hair'd villain.

FIRST MURDERER
What, you egg?

Stabbing him

Young fry of treachery.

SON
He has kill'd me, mother,
Run away I pray you.

Dies

LADY MACDUFF
Murder!

Exit LADY MACDUFF; the MURDERERS follow her

Act 4, Scene 3

Before the King's palace in England

Enter MALCOLM and MACDUFF

MACDUFF
Each new morn, new widows howl,
New sorrows strike heaven on the face,
That it resounds as if it felt with Scotland
And yell'd out like syllable of dolour.

MALCOLM
This tyrant, whose sole name blisters our tongues,
Was once thought honest.

MACDUFF
Bleed, bleed, poor country.

MALCOLM
I think our country sinks beneath the yoke,
It weeps, it bleeds, and each new day a gash
Is added to her wounds. I think withal,
There would be hands uplifted in my right:
And here from gracious England have I offer
Of goodly thousands:
Old Siward, with ten thousand warlike men,
Already at a point, was setting forth.
Now we'll together; and the chance of goodness
Be like our warranted quarrel.

Enter ROSS

MACDUFF
My ever gentle cousin, welcome hither.

MALCOLM
Good God, betimes remove
The means that makes us strangers.

ROSS
Sir, amen.

MACDUFF
Stands Scotland where it did?

ROSS
Alas, poor country, where groans and shrieks
That rend the air are made.

MALCOLM
Be't their comfort we are coming thither:
Gracious England hath lent us good Siward
And ten thousand men.

MACDUFF
What's the newest grief?
How does my wife?

ROSS
Let not your ears despise my tongue forever,
Which shall possess them with the heaviest sound
That ever yet they heard.

MACDUFF
I guess at it.

ROSS
Your castle is surprised: your wife and babes
Savagely slaughter'd.

MACDUFF
My children too?

ROSS
Wife, children, servants,
All that could be found.

MACDUFF
All my pretty ones?
Did you say all? O hell-kite! All?
What, all my pretty chickens, and their dam
At one fell swoop?

MALCOLM
Dispute it like a man.
Be this the whetstone of your sword, let grief
Convert to anger: blunt not the heart, enrage it.

MACDUFF
Gentle heavens,
Cut short all intermission: front to front
Bring thou this fiend of Scotland, and myself
Within my sword's length set him.

MALCOLM
This time goes manly:
Come, go we to the king, our power is ready,
Our lack is nothing but our leave. Macbeth
Is ripe for shaking, and the powers above
Put on their instruments: receive what cheer you may,
The night is long that never finds the day.

Exeunt

ACT 5, SCENE 1

AN ANTE-ROOM IN MACBETH'S CASTLE

Enter a DOCTOR and a GENTLEWOMAN

DOCTOR
When was it she last walk'd?

GENTLEWOMAN
Since his majesty went into the field, I have seen
Her rise from her bed, throw her night-gown upon
Her, unlock her closet, take forth paper, fold it,
Write upon't, read it, afterwards seal it, and again
Return to bed; yet all this while in a most fast sleep.

DOCTOR
A great perturbation in nature, to receive at once
The benefit of sleep, and do the effects of watching.

Enter LADY MACBETH with a taper

GENTLEWOMAN
Lo you, here she comes: this is her very guise,
And upon my life fast asleep.

DOCTOR
What is it she does now?
Look, how she rubs her hands.

GENTLEWOMAN
It is an accustomed action with her,
To seem thus washing her hands.

LADY MACBETH
Yet here's a spot.

DOCTOR
Hark, she speaks.

LADY MACBETH
Out, damned spot: out, I say. One: two: why,
Then, 'tis time to do't. Hell is murky. Fie, my
Lord, fie, a soldier, and afeard? What need we
Fear who knows it, when none can call our power to
Account? Yet who would have thought the old man
To have had so much blood in him.
The Thane of Fife had a wife: where is she now?
What, will these hands ne'er be clean?
Here's the smell of the blood still: all the
Perfumes of Arabia will not sweeten this little hand.

DOCTOR
This disease is beyond my practise: yet I have known
Those which have walked in their sleep who have died
Holily in their beds.

LADY MACBETH
Wash your hands, put on your nightgown, look not so
Pale: I tell you yet again Banquo's buried;
To bed, to bed. There's knocking at the gate:
Come, come, come, come, give me your hand. What's
Done cannot be undone. To bed, to bed, to bed.

Exit

DOCTOR
Foul whisp'rings are abroad: unnatural deeds
Do breed unnatural troubles:
More needs she the divine, than the physician.
God, God forgive us all.

Exeunt

Act 5, Scene 2

The country near Dunsinane

***Drum and colours. Enter MENTEITH, CAITHNESS and
ANGUS***

MENTEITH
The English power is near, led on by Malcolm,
His uncle Siward, and the good Macduff.
Revenges burn in them.

ANGUS
Near Birnam wood shall we well meet them.
I have a file of all the gentry: there is Siward's son,
And many unrough youths that even now
Protest their first of manhood.

MENTEITH
What does the tyrant?

CAITHNESS
Great Dunsinane he strongly fortifies:
Some say he's mad: others, that lesser hate him,
Do call it valiant fury.

ANGUS
Now does he feel
His secret murders sticking on his hands;
Those he commands, move only in command,
Nothing in love: now does he feel his title
Hang loose about him.

CAITHNESS
March we on:
Meet we the medicine of the sickly weal,
And with him pour we in our country's purge,
Each drop of us.

ANGUS
Or so much as it needs,
To dew the sovereign flower, and drown the weeds:
Make we our march towards Birnam.

Exeunt

ACT 5, SCENE 3

A ROOM IN MACBETH'S CASTLE

Enter MACBETH and SEYTON

MACBETH
Till Birnam wood remove to Dunsinane,
I cannot taint with fear. What's the boy Malcolm?
Was he not born of woman? The spirits that know
All mortal consequences, have pronounced me thus:
'Fear not, Macbeth, no man that's born of woman
Shall e'er have power upon thee.' Then fly, false thanes,
And mingle with the English epicures,
The mind I sway by and the heart I bear,
Shall never sag with doubt, nor shake with fear.

SEYTON
There is ten thousand soldiers, sir.

MACBETH
What soldiers? Death of thy soul.
Those linen cheeks of thine are counsellors to fear.
What soldiers?

SEYTON
The English force, so please you.

MACBETH
I am sick at heart; I have lived long enough:
That which should accompany old age,
As honour, love, obedience, troops of friends,
I must not look to have.
I'll fight till from my bones my flesh be hack'd.

Give me my armour. The thanes fly from me.
Skirr the country round; hang those that talk of fear.
I will not be afraid of death and bane,
Till Birnam forest come to Dunsinane.

Exeunt

Act 5, Scene 4

Country near Birnam wood

Drum and colours. Enter MALCOLM, SIWARD, MACDUFF, MENTEITH, CAITHNESS and ANGUS

MALCOLM
Cousins, I hope the days are near at hand
That chambers will be safe.

MENTEITH
We doubt it nothing.

SIWARD
What wood is this before us?

CAITHNESS
The wood of Birnam.

MALCOLM
Let every soldier hew him down a bough,
And bear't before him, thereby shall we shadow
The numbers of our host and make discovery
Err in report of us.

SIWARD
We learn no other, but the confident tyrant
Keeps still in Dunsinane, and will endure
Our setting down before't.

MALCOLM
'Tis his main hope:
For where there is advantage to be given,
Both more and less have given him the revolt,

And none serve with him, but constrained things,
Whose hearts are absent too.

ANGUS
Let our just censures
Attend the true event, and put we on
Industrious soldiership.

SIWARD
The time approaches,
That will with due decision make us know
What we shall say we have, and what we owe:
Thoughts speculative, their unsure hopes relate,
But certain issue, strokes must arbitrate,
Towards which, advance the war.

MACDUFF
Make all our trumpets speak; give them all breath,
Those clamorous harbingers of blood and death.

Exeunt

ACT 5, SCENE 5

WITHIN MACBETH'S CASTLE

Enter MACBETH and SEYTON

MACBETH
Hang out our banners on the outward walls,
The cry is still, 'They come:' our castle's strength
Will laugh a siege to scorn: here let them lie,
Till famine and the ague eat them up:
Were they not forced with those that should be ours,
We might have met them dareful, beard to beard,
And beat them backward home.

A cry within

What is that noise?

SEYTON
It is the cry of women, my good lord.

Exit

MACBETH
I have almost forgot the taste of fears:
The time has been, my senses would have cool'd
To hear a night-shriek;
Direness familiar to my slaughterous thoughts
Cannot once start me.

Re-enter SEYTON

SEYTON
The queen (my lord) is dead.

MACBETH
She should have died hereafter;
There would have been a time for such a word:
Tomorrow, and tomorrow, and tomorrow,
Creeps in this petty pace from day to day,
To the last syllable of recorded time:
And all our yesterdays, have lighted fools
The way to dusty death. Out, out, brief candle,
Life's but a walking shadow, a poor player,
That struts and frets his hour upon the stage,
And then is heard no more. It is a tale
Told by an idiot, full of sound and fury,
Signifying nothing.

SEYTON
As I did stand my watch upon the hill,
I look'd toward Birnam, and anon methought,
The wood began to move.

MACBETH
If thou speak'st false,
Upon the next tree shalt thou hang alive,
Till famine cling thee:
'Fear not, till Birnam wood
Do come to Dunsinane,' and now a wood
Comes toward Dunsinane. Arm, arm, and out,
If this which he avouches does appear,
There is nor flying hence, nor tarrying here.
I 'gin to be aweary of the sun,
And wish the estate o'th'world were now undone.

Alarums

I cannot fly, but, bear-like, I must fight the course.
What's he that was not born of woman?
Such a one am I to fear, or none.

146

Enter MACDUFF

Of all men else I have avoided thee:
But get thee back, my soul is too much charg'd
With blood of thine already.

MACDUFF
My voice is in my sword, thou bloodier villain
Than terms can give thee out.

MACBETH
I bear a charmed life, which must not yield,
To one of woman born.

MACDUFF
Despair thy charm;
Macduff was from his mother's womb
Untimely ripp'd.

MACBETH
Accursed be that tongue that tells me so.

MACDUFF
Yield thee, coward;
We'll have thee painted on a pole,
And underwrit, 'Here may you see the tyrant.'

MACBETH
I will not yield
To kiss the ground before young Malcolm's feet,
And to be baited with the rabble's curse.
Before my body, I throw my warlike shield.
Lay on, Macduff, and damn'd be him
That first cries, 'Hold, enough!'

Exeunt, fighting. Alarums. Battle sounds

ACT 5, SCENE 6

THE APPROACH TO MACBETH'S CASTLE

Flourish. Enter, with drum and colours, MALCOLM, SIWARD, MENTEITH, CAITHNESS and ANGUS

SIWARD
This way, my lord; the castle's gently render'd:
The noble thanes do bravely in the war,
The day almost itself professes yours,
And little is to do.

MALCOLM
We have met with foes that strike beside us.
I would the friends we miss, were safe arrived.

ANGUS
Some must go off: and yet, by these I see,
So great a day as this is cheaply bought.
Here comes newer comfort.

Enter MACDUFF with MACBETH's head

MACDUFF
Hail king, for so thou art.
Behold, where stands
Th'usurper's cursed head: the time is free:
I see thee compass'd with thy kingdom's pearl,
That speak my salutation in their minds:
Whose voices I desire aloud with mine.
Hail, King of Scotland.

ALL
Hail, King of Scotland.

Flourish

MALCOLM
We shall not spend a large expense of time,
Before we reckon with your several loves,
And make us even with you. My thanes and kinsmen
Henceforth be earls, the first that ever Scotland
In such an honour nam'd. What's more to do,
Which would be planted newly with the time,
As calling home our exil'd friends abroad,
That fled the snares of watchful tyranny,
Producing forth the cruel ministers
Of this dead butcher and his fiend-like queen;
Who (as 'tis thought) by self and violent hands,
Took off her life. This, and what needful else
That calls upon us, by the grace of Grace,
We will perform in measure, time, and place:
So thanks to all at once and to each one,
Whom we invite to see us crown'd at Scone.

Flourish. Exeunt

Julius Caesar

INTRODUCTION

With its betrayal, murder and suicide, *Julius Caesar* has a good number of the elements key to making a play attractive to an audience keen on sensation. This abridged version retains the play's core plot and its most famous speeches, while streamlining some of the less central features. You will not find Cassius and Brutus falling out here, for example, nor are there quite so many conspirators as in Shakespeare's original play. At first, the Chorus provides the voice of a republican citizenry, alarmed by Caesar's vain drift towards tyranny, and baying for his blood. But then, manipulated by Mark Antony's ingenious rhetoric – kept here pretty much in its entirety – the Chorus turns on Brutus, Cassius and their co-conspirators. The final battle at Philippi (42BC) is briefer than that in the original play, but there is still time and opportunity for the conspirators to die by their own hands.

SYNOPSIS

The people of Rome rejoice as Julius Caesar makes a triumphal entry into Rome. Yet there are those, led in this version by the Chorus, who see Caesar's elevation above other citizens as a danger: a leader who might put his citizens in servitude threatens the republic. Caesar encounters a soothsayer who warns him to 'beware the Ides of March'. Cassius notes that Brutus has been unsettled of late, a disposition that is worsened when there are shouts from the citizenry that suggest Caesar has been made king. Casca tells Brutus that Mark Antony has indeed offered Caesar the crown, though Caesar has refused it.

Rome's sky is disturbed by portentous weather. There is further talk that the senators plan to make Caesar king. Cassius and his co-conspirators begin their plan to ensure that Caesar will not live long enough to be made the offer. The next day, Calpurnia implores Caesar not to attend the senate house, worried that the portents foretell Caesar's demise. The conspirators persuade Caesar to attend, on the Ides of March. At the senate house, Mark Antony is taken to one side, to enable the conspirators easy access to Caesar. They begin petitioning for Caesar to overturn the banishment of Cinna's brother. While Caesar is refusing, the conspirators stab him to death.

Mark Antony meets with Brutus and Cassius, unsure of whether he too will be assassinated. He is assured that he is safe, as he insists that he is a friend of the conspirators. Mark Antony requests, however, that he be allowed to speak at Caesar's funeral. Brutus allows this, but only so long as Brutus himself speaks first, Mark Antony does not criticise the conspirators, and he makes it clear that Brutus and Cassius have allowed him to praise Caesar.

Mark Antony does indeed praise Caesar and, it seems, Brutus and Cassius. But, through his skilful rhetoric, Mark Antony manages to persuade the formerly bloodthirsty citizenry – the Chorus in this adaptation – that Brutus and Cassius are not 'honourable', but are murderers and villains. Brutus and Cassius flee from Rome, afraid that those avenging Caesar's death will murder them.

Cassius and Brutus worry that they will be overcome by the powerful military forces of Mark Antony and Octavius Caesar. They discuss military tactics, before the ghost of Caesar appears to Brutus, informing him that that he will appear again at Philippi – the place of battle. Brutus and Cassius parley with Mark Antony and Octavius, but it is resolved that they will fight. Pindarus wrongly informs Cassius that Titinius, Cassius's friend and general, has been surrounded and taken by enemy troops. At Cassius's own request, he is killed by Pindarus. Cassius's body is discovered, and Titinius kills himself next to it. Brutus finds the bodies of Cassius and Titinius. Brutus asks Strato to hold his sword while Brutus kills himself by running upon it. Mark Antony and Octavius arrive to find the bodies; Mark Antony describes Brutus as 'the noblest Roman of them all', as he killed Caesar for what he thought was the common good of Rome, not because of his own jealousy.

CAST
(in order of appearance)

Chorus
Flavius
First Commoner
Marullus
Second Commoner
Soothsayer
Julius Caesar
Brutus
Cassius
Mark Antony
Casca
Cicero
Cinna
Lucius
Decius Brutus
Calpurnia
Trebonius
Octavius Caesar
Messala
Titinius
Pindarus
Volumnius
Cato
Strato

PROLOGUE

CHORUS
Wherefore rejoice?
What conquest brings Caesar home?
What tributaries follow him to Rome,
To grace in captive bonds his chariot wheels?
O you hard hearts,
You cruel men of Rome,
Knew you not Pompey?
Many a time and oft have you climb'd up
To walls and battlements,
To towers and windows,
Yea, to chimney-tops,
Your infants in your arms,
And there have sat the live-long day,
With patient expectation,
To see great Pompey pass the streets of Rome:
And when you saw his chariot but appear,
Have you not made an universal shout,
That Tiber trembled underneath her banks,
To hear the replication of your sounds
Made in her concave shores?
And do you now put on your best attire?
And do you now cull out a holiday?
And do you now strew flowers in his way,
That comes in triumph over Pompey's blood?
Run to your houses, fall upon your knees,
Pray to the gods to intermit the plague
That needs must light on this ingratitude.

Act 1, Scene 1

A street in Rome

Enter FLAVIUS, MARULLUS and TWO COMMONERS

FLAVIUS
Hence: home, you idle creatures, get you home:
Is this a holiday? Speak, what trade art thou?

FIRST COMMONER
Why, sir, a carpenter. We make holiday,
To see Caesar and to rejoice in his triumph.

MARULLUS
You, sir, what trade are you?

SECOND COMMONER
I am but, as you would say, a cobbler.
A trade, sir, that, I hope, I may use with a safe
Conscience, which is, indeed, sir, a mender of bad soles.
I am, sir, a surgeon to old shoes:
When they are in great danger, I recover them.

FLAVIUS
Go, go, good countrymen, and for this fault
Assemble all the poor men of your sort;
Draw them to Tiber banks, and weep your tears
Into the channel.

Exeunt COMMONERS

See where their basest metal be not mov'd,
They vanish tongue-tied in their guiltiness:

Go you down that way towards the Capitol,
This way will I: disrobe the images,
If you do find them deck'd with ceremonies.

MARULLUS
May we do so?
You know it is the feast of Lupercal.

FLAVIUS
It is no matter; let no images
Be hung with Caesar's trophies: I'll about,
And drive away the vulgar from the streets;
These growing feathers, pluck'd from Caesar's wing,
Will make him fly an ordinary pitch,
Who else would soar above the view of men,
And keep us all in servile fearfulness.

Exeunt

ACT 1, SCENE 2

A PUBLIC PLACE

Flourish. Enter SOOTHSAYER, CAESAR, BRUTUS, CASSIUS and CASCA

SOOTHSAYER
Caesar.

CAESAR
I hear a tongue, shriller than all the music
Cry 'Caesar': speak, Caesar is turn'd to hear.

SOOTHSAYER
Beware the Ides of March.

CAESAR
What man is that?

BRUTUS
A soothsayer bids you beware the Ides of March.

CAESAR
What say'st thou to me now? Speak once again.

SOOTHSAYER
Beware the Ides of March.

CAESAR
He is a dreamer, let us leave him: pass.

Sennet. Exeunt all but BRUTUS and CASSIUS

CASSIUS
Brutus, I do observe you now of late:
I have not from your eyes that gentleness
And show of love, as I was wont to have.

BRUTUS
Vexed I am of late, with passions of some difference,
Conceptions only proper to myself,
Which give some soil (perhaps) to my behaviours:
But let not therefore my good friends be grieved
(Among which number, Cassius, be you one).

CASSIUS
Then Brutus, I have much mistook your passion,
By means whereof, this breast of mine hath buried
Thoughts of great value, worthy cogitations.
Tell me, good Brutus, can you see your face?
It is very much lamented Brutus,
That you have no such mirrors, as will turn
Your hidden worthiness into your eye,
That you might see your shadow: I have heard,
Where many of the best respect in Rome,
(Except immortal Caesar) speaking of Brutus,
And groaning underneath this age's yoke,
Have wish'd, that noble Brutus had his eyes.

BRUTUS
Into what dangers would you lead me Cassius,
That you would have me seek into myself,
For that which is not in me?

CASSIUS
Good Brutus, be prepared to hear:
And since you know you cannot see yourself
So well as by reflection; I your glass,
Will modestly discover to yourself
That of yourself, which you yet know not of.

Shout. Flourish

BRUTUS
What means this shouting?
I do fear, the people choose Caesar
For their king.

CASSIUS
Ay, do you fear it?
Then must I think you would not have it so.

BRUTUS
I would not, Cassius, yet I love him well:
But wherefore do you hold me here so long?
What is it that you would impart to me?

CHORUS
We were born free as Caesar,
So were you,
We all have fed as well,
And we can all endure the winter's cold as well as he.
For once, upon a raw and gusty day,
The troubled Tiber, chafing with her shores,
Caesar said to us:
'Darest thou, now leap in with me into this angry flood,
And swim to yonder point?'
Upon the word, we plunged in and bad him follow:
So indeed he did.
The torrent roar'd,
And we did buffet it with lusty sinews,
Throwing it aside,
And stemming it with hearts of controversy.
But ere we could arrive the point propos'd,
Caesar cried, 'Help me, or I sink!'
We (as Aeneas, our great ancestor,
Did from the flames of Troy

Upon his shoulder the old Anchises bear)
So from the waves of Tiber did we the tired Caesar:
And this man is now become a god,
And we are wretched creatures
And must bend our bodies,
If Caesar carelessly but nod on us.
Ye gods, it doth amaze us a man of such a feeble temper
Should so get the start of the majestic world,
And bear the palm alone.
He doth bestride the narrow world like a Colossus,
And we petty men walk under his huge legs
And peep about to find ourselves dishonourable graves.
Upon what meat doth this our Caesar feed,
That he is grown so great?
Age, thou art sham'd.
Rome, thou hast lost the breed of noble bloods.
When went there by an age, since the great flood,
But it was fam'd with more than with one man?
When could they say (till now) that talk'd of Rome,
That her wide walls encompass'd but one man?
Now is it Rome indeed, and room enough,
When there is in it but one only man.

Shout. Flourish

BRUTUS
I do believe, that these applauses are
For some new honours, that are heap'd on Caesar.

CASSIUS
The fault (dear Brutus) is not in our stars,
But in ourselves, that we are underlings.
Brutus and Caesar: what should be in that Caesar?
Why should that name be sounded more than yours?
O! You and I, have heard our fathers say,
There was a Brutus once that would have brook'd

Th'eternal devil to keep his state in Rome
As easily as a king.

BRUTUS
That you do love me, I am nothing jealous:
What you would work me to, I have some aim:
How I have thought of this, and of these times
I shall recount hereafter; what you have said,
I will consider: what you have to say
I will with patience hear.
Brutus had rather be a villager
Than to repute himself a son of Rome
Under these hard conditions, as this time
Is like to lay upon us.

CASSIUS
I am glad that my weak words
Have struck but thus much show of fire from Brutus.

BRUTUS
The games are done,
And Caesar is returning.

Re-enter CAESAR, ANTONY and CASCA

CAESAR
Antony.

ANTONY
Caesar?

CAESAR
Let me have men about me, that are fat,
Sleek-headed men and such as sleep a-nights:
Yond Cassius has a lean and hungry look,
He thinks too much: such men are dangerous.

He reads much, he is a great observer and he looks
Quite through the deeds of men. He loves no plays,
As thou dost Antony; he hears no music;
Seldom he smiles. Such men as he be never at heart's ease,
Whiles they behold a greater than themselves,
And therefore are they very dangerous.

Sennet. Exeunt CAESAR and ANTONY

BRUTUS
Casca, tell us what hath chanc'd today,
That Caesar looks so sad.

CASCA
I saw Mark Antony offer him a crown,
'Twas one of these coronets:
And he put it by once: but, for all that, to my
Thinking, he would fain have had it. Then he
Offered it to him again: then he put it by again:
But to my thinking, he was very loath to lay his
Fingers off it. And then he offered it the third
Time; he put it the third time by, and still as he
Refus'd it, the rabblement hooted, and clap'd their
Chapped hands, and uttered such a deal of stinking breath
Because Caesar refus'd the crown that it had (almost) choked
Caesar: for he swooned and fell down at it.

BRUTUS
What said he, when he came unto himself?

CASCA
When he came to himself again, he said,
If he had done, or said any thing amiss, he desir'd
Their worships to think it was his infirmity.

CASSIUS
Did Cicero say any thing?

CASCA
Ay, those that understood him smil'd at
One another and shook their heads; but, for mine own
Part, it was Greek to me. I could tell you more
News too: Marullus and Flavius, for pulling scarfs
Off Caesar's images, are put to silence.

CASSIUS
Will you dine with me tomorrow, Casca?

CASCA
Ay, farewell, both.

Exit

BRUTUS
For this time I will leave you:
Tomorrow, if you please to speak with me,
I will come home to you: or if you will,
Come home to me, and I will wait for you.

CASSIUS
I will do so: till then, think of the world.

Exit BRUTUS

Well, Brutus, thou art noble: yet I see,
Thy honourable metal may be wrought
From that it is dispos'd: therefore it is meet,
That noble minds keep ever with their likes:
For who so firm, that cannot be seduced?

Exit

ACT 1, SCENE 3

THE SAME

Thunder

CHORUS
We have seen tempests,
When the scolding winds have riv'd the knotty oaks,
And we have seen th'ambitious ocean
Swell, and rage, and foam,
To be exalted with the threatening clouds:
But never till tonight, never till now,
Did we go through a tempest-dropping-fire.
Either there is a civil strife in heaven,
Or else the world, too saucy with the gods,
Incenses them to send destruction.
A common slave held up his left hand,
Which did flame and burn like twenty torches join'd;
And yet his hand, not sensible of fire, remain'd unscorch'd.
Against the Capitol we met a lion,
Who glar'd upon us, and went surly by, without annoying us.
And there were drawn upon a heap, a hundred ghastly women,
Transformed with their fear,
Who swore they saw men, all in fire, walk up and down the streets.
And yesterday, the bird of night did sit even at noon-day
Upon the market place, hooting, and shrieking.
When these prodigies do so conjointly meet,
Let not men say 'These are their reasons, they are natural:'
For we believe, they are portentous things
Unto the climate, that they point upon.

Enter CASCA and CICERO

CICERO
It is a strange disposed time:
But men may construe things after their fashion,
Clean from the purpose of the things themselves.
Comes Caesar to the Capitol tomorrow?

CASCA
He doth.

CICERO
Goodnight then, Casca:
This disturbed sky is not to walk in.

Exit CICERO. Enter CASSIUS

CASCA
Cassius, whoever knew the heavens menace so?

CASSIUS
Those that have known the earth so full of faults.

CASCA
It is the part of men, to fear and tremble,
When the most mighty gods, by tokens send
Such dreadful heralds, to astonish us.

CASSIUS
If you would consider the true cause,
Why all things change from their ordinance,
Their natures, and pre-formed faculties,
To monstrous quality; why you shall find,
That heaven hath infus'd them with these spirits,
To make them instruments of fear, and warning,
Unto some monstrous state.
Now could I (Casca) name to thee a man,
Most like this dreadful night,

That thunders, lightens, opens graves, and roars,
As doth the lion in the Capitol:
A man no mightier than thyself, or me,
In personal action; yet prodigious grown,
And fearful, as these strange eruptions are.

CASCA
'Tis Caesar that you mean:
Is it not, Cassius?

CASSIUS
Let it be who it is.

CASCA
They say, the senators tomorrow
Mean to establish Caesar as a king.

CASSIUS
I know where I will wear this dagger then;
Cassius from bondage will deliver Cassius.

CASCA
So every bondman in his own hand bears
The power to cancel his captivity.

CASSIUS
And why should Caesar be a tyrant then?
Poor man, I know he would not be a wolf,
But that he sees the Romans are but sheep:
What trash is Rome? What rubbish, and what offal?
When it serves for the base matter to illuminate
So vile a thing as Caesar.
Now know you, Casca, I have mov'd already
Some certain of the noblest minded Romans
To undergo, with me, an enterprise,

Of honourable dangerous consequence;
And I do know by this, they stay for me
In Pompey's porch.

CASCA
Stand close awhile, for here comes one in haste.
I will set this foot of mine as far
As who goes farthest.
'Tis Cinna, I do know him by his gait,
He is a friend.

Enter CINNA

CINNA
What a fearful night is this?
O Cassius, if you could
But win the noble Brutus to our party.

CASSIUS
Be you content. Good Cinna, take this paper,
And look you lay it in the praetor's chair,
Where Brutus may but find it: and throw this
In at his window; set this up with wax
Upon old Brutus' statue: all this done,
Repair to Pompey's porch, where you shall find us.

CINNA
I will hie, and so bestow these papers as you bad me.

Exit CINNA

CASSIUS
Come Casca, you and I will see Brutus at his house:
Three parts of him is ours already.

CASCA
O, he sits high in all the people's hearts:
And that which would appear offence in us,
His countenance, like richest alchemy,
Will change to virtue, and to worthiness.

CASSIUS
Him, and his worth, and our great need of him,
You have right well conceited: let us go,
For it is after midnight, and ere day
We will awake him, and be sure of him.

Exeunt

ACT 2, SCENE 1

BRUTUS'S ORCHARD

Enter BRUTUS

BRUTUS
It must be by his death: and for my part,
I know no personal cause, to spurn at him,
But for the general. He would be crown'd:
How that might change his nature, there's the question?
It is the bright day, that brings forth the adder,
And that craves wary walking: crown him that,
And then I grant we put a sting in him,
That at his will he may do danger with.
The abuse of greatness, is, when it disjoins
Remorse from power: 'tis a common proof,
That lowliness is young ambition's ladder,
Whereto the climber upward turns his face:
But when he once attains the upmost round,
He then unto the ladder turns his back,
Looks in the clouds, scorning the base degrees
By which he did ascend: so Caesar may.

Enter LUCIUS

LUCIUS
Sir: searching the window for a flint, I found
This paper, thus seal'd up.

Gives him the paper

BRUTUS
Is not tomorrow (boy) the Ides of March?
Look in the calendar, and bring me word.

LUCIUS
I will, sir.

Exit

BRUTUS
The exhalations, whizzing in the air
Give so much light, that I may read by them.

Opens the paper and reads

CHORUS
Brutus, thou sleep'st;
Awake, and see thyself:
Speak, strike, redress.
Brutus, thou sleep'st;
Awake.
Shall Rome stand under one man's awe?
What, Rome?
Your ancestors did from the streets of Rome
The Tarquin drive, when he was call'd a king.
Speak, strike, redress.

BRUTUS
O Rome, I make thee promise,
If the redress will follow, thou receivest
Thy full petition at the hand of Brutus.

Enter CASSIUS, CASCA, DECIUS BRUTUS and CINNA

CASSIUS
Good morrow Brutus, do we trouble you?

BRUTUS
I have been up this hour, awake all night:
Know I these men that come along with you?

CASSIUS
Yes, every man of them; and no man here
But honours you: this is Decius Brutus;
This, Casca; and this, Cinna.

BRUTUS
They are all welcome.

CHORUS
Speak, strike, redress!
Speak, strike, redress!
Speak, strike, redress!

CASCA
Let us swear our resolution.

BRUTUS
No, not an oath: if these,
(As I am sure they do) bear fire enough
To kindle cowards, and to steel with valour
The melting spirits of women, then, countrymen,
What need we any spur, but our own cause
To prick us to redress? What other oath
Than honesty to honesty engag'd,
That this shall be, or we will fall for it?
Do not stain the even virtue of our enterprise,
Nor th'insuppressive mettle of our spirits,
To think that, or our cause, or our performance
Did need an oath.

CINNA
Shall no man else be touch'd, but only Caesar?

CASSIUS
I think it is not meet, Mark Antony,
So well belov'd of Caesar, should out-live Caesar.

BRUTUS
Think not of him: for he can do no more
Than Caesar's arm when Caesar's head is off.
Our course will seem too bloody,
To cut the head off, and then hack the limbs:
Let's be sacrificers, but not butchers:
We all stand up against the spirit of Caesar,
And in the spirit of men, there is no blood:
Friends, let's kill him boldly, but not wrathfully:
And let our hearts, as subtle masters do,
Stir up their servants to an act of rage,
And after seem to chide 'em. This shall make
Our purpose necessary, and not envious.

Bell tolls

DECIUS BRUTUS
'Tis time to part.

CASSIUS
But it is doubtful yet,
Whether Caesar will come forth today:
For he is superstitious grown of late.
It may be, these apparent prodigies,
May hold him from the Capitol today.

DECIUS BRUTUS
If he be so resolv'd, I can o'ersway him;
I will bring him to the Capitol.

CASSIUS
Nay, we will all of us, be there to fetch him.
We'll leave you Brutus,
And friends disperse yourselves.

Exeunt

CHORUS

All remember what you have said,
And show yourselves true Romans.
Look fresh and merrily,
Let not your looks put on your purposes,
But bear it as our Roman actors do,
With untir'd spirits and formal constancy.
A lioness hath whelped in the streets,
Graves have yawn'd, and yielded up their dead;
Fierce fiery warriors fought upon the clouds
In ranks and squadrons, and right form of war
Which drizzl'd blood upon the Capitol:
The noise of battle hurtled in the air:
Horses did neigh, and dying men did groan,
And ghosts did shriek and squeal about the streets.
The heavens themselves blaze forth the death of princes.

Act 2, Scene 2

Caesar's house

Thunder. Enter CAESAR

CAESAR
Nor heaven, nor earth,
Have been at peace tonight:
Thrice hath Calpurnia, in her sleep cried out,
'Help, ho! They murder Caesar!'

Enter CALPURNIA

CALPURNIA
What mean you, Caesar? Think you to walk forth?
You shall not stir out of your house today.

CAESAR
Caesar shall forth; the things that threaten'd me
Ne'er look'd but on my back: when they shall see
The face of Caesar, they are vanished.

CALPURNIA
Caesar, I never stood on ceremonies,
Yet now they fright me: There is one within,
Besides the things that we have heard and seen,
Recounts most horrid sights seen by the watch.

CAESAR
Caesar shall go forth: for these predictions
Are to the world in general, as to Caesar.
Cowards die many times before their deaths,
The valiant never taste of death but once:

Caesar should be a beast without a heart
If he should stay at home today for fear.

CALPURNIA
Do not go forth today:
We'll send Mark Antony to the senate house,
And he shall say, you are not well today.

Enter DECIUS BRUTUS

Here's Decius Brutus, he shall tell them so.

DECIUS BRUTUS
Caesar, all hail: I come to fetch you to the senate house.

CAESAR
And you are come in very happy time,
To bear my greeting to the senators
And tell them that I will not come today.

DECIUS BRUTUS
Most mighty Caesar, let me know some cause.

CAESAR
The cause is in my will: I will not come,
That is enough to satisfy the senate.

CALPURNIA
Say he is sick.

DECIUS BRUTUS
The senate have concluded
To give this day, a crown to mighty Caesar.
If you shall send them word you will not come,
Their minds may change.

If Caesar hide himself, shall they not whisper
'Lo, Caesar is afraid'?
Pardon me, Caesar; for my dear dear love
To our proceeding, bids me tell you this:
And reason to my love is liable.

Enter BRUTUS, CASCA and CINNA

CAESAR
And look where Casca is come to fetch me.
Give me my robe, for I will go.

CASCA
Good morrow, Caesar.

CAESAR
Welcome Casca.
What Brutus, are you stirr'd so early too?
Good morrow, Cinna.
Bid them prepare within:
I am to blame to be thus waited for.
Now Cinna: I have an hour's talk in store for you:
Remember that you call on me today:
Be near me, that I may remember you.

CINNA
Caesar, I will:
[Aside] And so near will I be,
That your best friends shall wish I had been further.

CAESAR
Good friends, go in, and taste some wine with me.
And we (like friends) will straightway go together.

Exeunt

CHORUS
Caesar, beware of Brutus;
Take heed of Cassius;
Come not near Casca;
Have an eye to Cinna,
Decius Brutus loves thee not:
There is but one mind in all these men,
And it is bent against Caesar.

Act 3, Scene 1

In front of the Capitol

Flourish. Enter SOOTHSAYER, CAESAR, BRUTUS, CASSIUS, CASCA, DECIUS BRUTUS, TREBONIUS, CINNA and ANTONY

CAESAR
The Ides of March are come.

SOOTHSAYER
Ay Caesar, but not gone.

CAESAR goes to the senate house; the rest follow. TREBONIUS takes ANTONY to the side

CASSIUS
Trebonius knows his time: for look you Brutus
He draws Mark Antony out of the way.

DECIUS BRUTUS
Where is Cinna? Let him go,
And presently prefer his suit to Caesar.

BRUTUS
He is address'd: press near, and second him.

CINNA
Casca, you are the first that rears your hand.

CAESAR
Are we all ready? What is now amiss,
That Caesar and his senate must redress?

CINNA
Most high, most mighty, and most puissant Caesar,
Cinna throws before thy seat
An humble heart.

Kneeling

CAESAR
I must prevent thee, Cinna:
Thy brother by decree is banished:
If thou dost bend, and pray, and fawn for him,
I spurn thee like a cur out of my way.

CINNA
Is there no voice more worthy than my own,
To sound more sweetly in great Caesar's ear
For the repealing of my banish'd brother?

BRUTUS
I kiss thy hand, but not in flattery Caesar:
Desiring thee, that his brother may
Have an immediate freedom of repeal.

CASSIUS
Pardon, Caesar; Caesar, pardon:
As low as to thy foot doth Cassius fall,
To beg enfranchisement for Cinna's brother.

CAESAR
I am constant as the northern star.
The skies are painted with unnumber'd sparks,
They are all fire, and every one doth shine:
But, there's but one in all doth hold his place.
So in the world; 'tis furnish'd well with men,
And men are flesh and blood, and apprehensive;
Yet in the number, I do know but one

That unassailable holds on his rank,
Unshak'd of motion: and that I am he.
I was constant Cinna should be banish'd,
And constant do remain to keep him so.

CINNA
O Caesar.

CAESAR
Hence: wilt thou lift up Olympus?

DECIUS BRUTUS
Great Caesar.

CAESAR
Doth not Brutus bootless kneel?

CASCA
Speak, hands for me.

They stab CAESAR

CAESAR
Et tu, Brute? Then fall Caesar.

Dies. Exeunt with the body

CHORUS
Liberty.
Freedom.
Tyranny is dead.
Run hence, proclaim, cry it about the streets.
Some to the common pulpits, and cry out
'Liberty, freedom, and enfranchisement!'
People and senators, be not affrighted;
Stoop, Romans, stoop,

And let us bathe our hands
In Caesar's blood up to the elbows,
And besmear our swords:
Then walk we forth,
Waving our red weapons o'er our heads,
Let's all cry 'Peace, freedom and liberty!'

Enter CASSIUS, TREBONIUS and BRUTUS

CASSIUS
Where is Antony?

TREBONIUS
Fled to his house amaz'd:
Men, wives, and children stare, cry out, and run
As it were doomsday.

BRUTUS
Fates, we will know your pleasures:
That we shall die we know, 'tis but the time
And drawing days out, that men stand upon.

CASSIUS
Every man away.
Brutus shall lead, and we will grace his heels
With the most boldest, and best hearts of Rome.

Enter ANTONY

BRUTUS
But here comes Antony.
Welcome, Mark Antony.

ANTONY
I know not gentlemen what you intend,
Who else must be let blood:

I do beseech ye, if you bear me hard,
Now, whilst your purpled hands do reek and smoke,
Fulfil your pleasure.
No place will please me so, no mean of death,
As here by Caesar, and by you cut off,
The choice and master spirits of this age.

BRUTUS
O Antony, beg not your death of us:
Though now we must appear bloody and cruel,
Our hearts you see not, they are pitiful:
And pity to the general wrong of Rome
Hath done this deed on Caesar. For your part, Antony,
Our arms in strength of malice, and our hearts
Of brothers' temper, do receive you in,
With all kind love, good thoughts, and reverence.

CASSIUS
Your voice shall be as strong as any man's,
In the disposing of new dignities.

BRUTUS
Only be patient, till we have appeas'd
The multitude, and then we will deliver you the cause,
Why I, that did love Caesar when I struck him,
Have thus proceeded.

ANTHONY
I doubt not of your wisdom.
My credit now stands on such slippery ground,
That one of two bad ways you must conceit me,
Either a coward, or a flatterer.
That I did love Caesar, 'tis true:
If then his spirit look upon us now,
Shall it not grieve him dearer than his death,
To see his Antony making his peace,

Shaking the bloody fingers of his foes?
Here wast he bay'd, brave hart,
Here didst he fall, and here his hunters stand.

CASSIUS
I blame you not for praising Caesar so.
But what compact mean you to have with us?
Will you be prick'd in number of our friends,
Or shall we on, and not depend on you?

ANTONY
Friends am I with you all and love you all,
Upon this hope, that you shall give me reasons,
Why, and wherein, Caesar was dangerous.
That's all I seek: and am moreover suitor, that I may
Produce his body to the market place,
And in the pulpit as becomes a friend,
Speak in the order of his funeral.

BRUTUS
You shall Mark Antony.

CASSIUS
[Aside to BRUTUS]
You know not what you do; do not consent
That Antony speak in his funeral:
Know you how much the people may be mov'd
By that which he will utter?

BRUTUS
I will myself into the pulpit first,
And show the reason of our Caesar's death.
Antony, you shall not in your funeral speech blame us,
But speak all good you can devise of Caesar,
And say you do't by our permission.

ANTONY
I do desire no more.

Exeunt all but ANTONY

ANTONY
O, pardon me, thou bleeding piece of earth:
That I am meek and gentle with these butchers.
Woe to the hand that shed this costly blood.
Over Caesar's wounds now do I prophesy,
A curse shall light upon the limbs of men;
Domestic fury, and fierce civil strife,
Shall cumber all the parts of Italy:
And Caesar's spirit ranging for revenge,
With Ate by his side, come hot from hell,
Shall in these confines, with a monarch's voice,
Cry 'Havoc,' and let slip the dogs of war.
Octavius lies tonight within seven leagues of Rome:
A mourning Rome, a dangerous Rome,
No Rome of safety for Octavius yet.

Exit

ACT 3, SCENE 2

THE FORUM

CHORUS
Romans, countrymen, and lovers,
Hear us for our cause,
And be silent, that you may hear:
Believe us for our honour,
And have respect to our honour,
That you may believe:
Censure us in your wisdom,
And awake your senses,
That you may the better judge.
If there be any dear friend of Caesar's,
To him we say,
That Brutus' love to Caesar
Was no less than his.
If then that friend demand
Why Brutus rose against Caesar,
This is our answer:
Not that he loved Caesar less,
But that he loved Rome more.
Had you rather Caesar were living
And die all slaves,
Than that Caesar were dead,
To live all free men?
As Caesar loved us,
We weep for him;
As he was fortunate,
We rejoice at it;
As he was valiant,
We honour him:
But, as he was ambitious,

He was slain.
There is tears for his love;
Joy for his fortune;
Honour for his valour;
And death for his ambition.
Who is here so base
That would be a bondman?
Who is here so rude
That would not be a Roman?
Who is here so vile
That will not love his country?
Live, Brutus! Live, live!
Bring him with triumph home unto his house.
Give him a statue with his ancestors.
This Caesar was a tyrant.
We are blest that Rome is rid of him.

Enter ANTONY

ANTONY
Friends, Romans, countrymen, lend me your ears:
I come to bury Caesar, not to praise him:
The evil that men do, lives after them,
The good is oft interred with their bones,
So let it be with Caesar. The noble Brutus,
Hath told you Caesar was ambitious:
If it were so, it was a grievous fault,
And grievously hath Caesar answer'd it.
Here, under leave of Brutus and the rest
(For Brutus is an honourable man,
So are they all; all honourable men)
Come I to speak in Caesar's funeral.
He was my friend, faithful, and just to me;
But Brutus says, he was ambitious,
And Brutus is an honourable man.
He hath brought many captives home to Rome,

Whose ransoms, did the general coffers fill:
Did this in Caesar seem ambitious?
When that the poor have cried, Caesar hath wept:
Ambition should be made of sterner stuff,
Yet Brutus says, he was ambitious:
And Brutus is an honourable man.
You all did see, that on the Lupercal,
I thrice presented him a kingly crown,
Which he did thrice refuse. Was this ambition?
Yet Brutus says, he was ambitious:
And sure he is an honourable man.
I speak not to disprove what Brutus spoke,
But here I am, to speak what I do know;
You all did love him once, not without cause,
What cause withholds you then, to mourn for him?
Bear with me, my heart is with Caesar,
And I must pause, till it come back to me.

CHORUS
There is much reason in his sayings.
If thou consider rightly of the matter,
Caesar has had great wrong.
I fear there will a worse come in his place.
He would not take the crown,
Therefore 'tis certain he was not ambitious.
If it be found so, some will dear abide it.
There's not a nobler man in Rome than Antony.
Now mark him, he begins again to speak.

ANTONY
O masters! If I were dispos'd to stir
Your hearts and minds to mutiny and rage,
I should do Brutus wrong, and Cassius wrong:
Who (you all know) are honourable men.
I will not do them wrong: I rather choose
To wrong the dead, to wrong myself and you,

Than I will wrong such honourable men.
But here's a parchment, with the seal of Caesar;
'Tis his will: let but the commons hear this testament:
(Which pardon me) I do not mean to read,
And they would go and kiss dead Caesar's wounds
And dip their napkins in his sacred blood.

CHORUS
We'll hear the will,
Read it, Mark Antony.
The will, the will;
We will hear Caesar's will.
You shall read us the will, Caesar's will.

ANTONY
Have patience gentle friends, I must not read it;
It is not meet you know how Caesar lov'd you:
You are but men, and, being men,
It will inflame you, it will make you mad:
'Tis good you know not that you are his heirs,
For if you should, O what would come of it?
I have o'ershot myself to tell you of it,
I fear I wrong the honourable men,
Whose daggers have stabb'd Caesar: I do fear it.

CHORUS
They were traitors:
Honourable men?
The will.
The testament.
They were villains,
Murderers:
The will.
Read the will.

ANTONY
You will compel me then to read the will:
To every Roman citizen he gives,
To every several man, seventy five drachmas.
Moreover, he hath left you all his walks,
His private arbours, and new-planted orchards,
On this side Tiber, he hath left them you,
And to your heirs for ever: common pleasures
To walk abroad, and recreate yourselves.
Here was a Caesar: when comes such another?
Brutus, as you know, was Caesar's angel.
Judge, O you gods, how dearly Caesar lov'd him:
This was the most unkindest cut of all.
For when the noble Caesar saw him stab,
Ingratitude, more strong than traitors' arms,
Quite vanquish'd him: then burst his mighty heart.

CHORUS
O noble Caesar!
O piteous spectacle!
O woeful day!
O traitors, villains!
O most bloody sight!
We will be reveng'd!
Let not a traitor live!
Revenge!
About!
Seek!
Burn!
Fire!
Kill!
Slay!

ANTONY
Good friends, sweet friends, let me not stir you up
To such a sudden flood of mutiny:
They that have done this deed, are honourable.
What private griefs they have, alas I know not,
That made them do it: they are wise, and honourable,
And will no doubt with reasons answer you.
I come not (friends) to steal away your hearts,
I am no orator, as Brutus is:
But (as you know me all) a plain blunt man
That love my friend, and that they know full well,
That gave me public leave to speak of him:
For I have neither wit nor words, nor worth,
Action, nor utterance, nor the power of speech,
To stir men's blood. I only speak right on:
I tell you that which you yourselves do know.

CHORUS
We'll mutiny.
We'll burn the house of Brutus.
Come, seek the conspirators.

Enter OCTAVIUS

OCTAVIUS
Brutus and Cassius are rid like madmen
Through the gates of Rome.

ANTONY
Belike they had some notice of the people
How I had moved them.
If Brutus and Cassius are levying powers:
We must straight make head:
Therefore let our alliance be combined,
Our best friends made, our means stretch'd
And let us presently go sit in council.

OCTAVIUS
Let us do so: for we are at the stake,
And bay'd about with many enemies;
And some that smile have in their hearts,
I fear, millions of mischiefs.

Exeunt

CHORUS
Most noble Caesar!
We'll revenge his death.
O royal Caesar!
Come, brands ho!
Fire-brands:
To Brutus',
To Cassius';
Burn all:
Some to Decius' house,
And some to Casca's;
Away, go!

ACT 4, SCENE 1

BRUTUS'S CAMP NEAR SARDIS

Drum. Enter CASSIUS and BRUTUS

CASSIUS
Come, Antony, and young Octavius come,
Revenge yourselves alone on Cassius,
For Cassius is a-weary of the world:
O I could weep my spirit from mine eyes.
There is my dagger, and here my naked breast:
Within, a heart richer than gold:
Strike, as thou didst at Caesar: for I know,
When thou didst hate him worst,
Thou lovedst him better
Than ever thou lovedst Cassius.

BRUTUS
Sheathe your dagger:
O Cassius, you are yoked with a lamb
That carries anger, as the flint bears fire,
Who, much enforced, shows a hasty spark,
And straight is cold again.
I am sick of many griefs.
I have here received letters,
That young Octavius and Mark Antony
Come down upon us with a mighty power,
Bending their expedition toward Philippi.
By proscription, and bills of outlawry,
Octavius and Antony,
Have put to death, an hundred senators.
What do you think of marching to Philippi presently?

CASSIUS
I do not think it good.
'Tis better that the enemy seek us,
So shall he waste his means, weary his soldiers,
Whilst we, lying still, are full of rest.

BRUTUS
Good reasons must of force give place to better:
The people 'twixt Philippi and this ground
Do stand but in a forced affection:
For they have grudged us contribution.
The enemy, marching along by them,
By them shall make a fuller number up,
Come on refresh'd, new added, and encourag'd:
From which advantage shall we cut him off.
You must note beside,
That we have tried the utmost of our friends:
Our legions are brim full, our cause is ripe,
The enemy increaseth every day,
We at the height, are ready to decline.
We must take the current when it serves,
Or lose our ventures.

CASSIUS
Then with your will go on:
We'll along ourselves, and meet them at Philippi.
Early tomorrow will we rise, and hence.
Good night, my lord.

Exit CASSIUS

BRUTUS
Good night, good brother.

BRUTUS rests. Enter GHOST OF CAESAR

How ill this taper burns. Ha! Who comes here?
I think it is the weakness of mine eyes
That shapes this monstrous apparition.
It comes upon me: art thou any thing?
Art thou some god, some angel, or some devil,
That mak'st my blood cold, and my hair to stare?
Speak to me, what thou art.

GHOST
Thy evil spirit, Brutus.

BRUTUS
Why com'st thou?

GHOST
To tell thee thou shalt see me at Philippi.

BRUTUS
Why, I will see thee at Philippi, then.

Exit GHOST OF CAESAR

Now I have taken heart thou vanishes.
Ill spirit, I would hold more talk with thee.

Exit

Act 4, Scene 2

The plains of Philippi

Enter OCTAVIUS and ANTONY

OCTAVIUS
Now Antony, our hopes are answered,
The enemy's battles are at hand,
They mean to warn us at Philippi here:
Answering before we do demand of them.

ANTONY
They could be content to visit other places,
And come down with fearful bravery:
Thinking by this face to fasten in our thoughts
That they have courage; but 'tis not so.

Drum. Enter BRUTUS and CASSIUS

BRUTUS
They stand, and would have parley.

OCTAVIUS
Mark Antony, shall we give sign of battle?

ANTONY
No Caesar, we will answer on their charge.

BRUTUS
Words before blows: is it so countrymen?

OCTAVIUS
Not that we love words better, as you do.

BRUTUS
Good words are better than bad strokes Octavius.

ANTONY
In your bad strokes, Brutus, you give good words.
Witness the hole you made in Caesar's heart,
Crying 'Long live! Hail, Caesar.'

CASSIUS
Antony,
The posture of your blows are yet unknown;
But for your words, they rob the Hybla bees,
And leave them honeyless.

ANTONY
Not stingless too.

BRUTUS
O yes, and soundless too.

OCTAVIUS
Come, come, the cause: if arguing make us sweat,
The proof of it will turn to redder drops.
Look, I draw a sword against conspirators,
When think you that the sword goes up again?
Never till Caesar's three and thirty wounds
Be well aveng'd; or till another Caesar
Have added slaughter to the sword of traitors.

BRUTUS
Caesar, thou canst not die by traitors' hands,
Unless thou bring'st them with thee.

OCTAVIUS
So I hope:
I was not born to die on Brutus' sword.

Come, Antony: away:
Defiance traitors, hurl we in your teeth.
If you dare fight today, come to the field;
If not, when you have stomachs.

CASSIUS
Come, ho! Away!

Exeunt

CHORUS
Why, now,
Blow wind,
Swell billow
And swim bark.
The storm is up,
And all is on the hazard.
O, that a man might know
The end of this day's business ere it come.
But it sufficeth that the day will end,
And then the end is known.

ACT 4, SCENE 3

THE FIELD OF BATTLE

Battle sounds. Alarums. Enter BRUTUS and MESSALA

BRUTUS
Ride, ride, Messala, ride, and give these bills
Unto the legions, on the other side.
Let them set on at once: for I perceive
But cold demeanor in Octavius' wing:
And sudden push gives them the overthrow.

Exeunt. Battle sounds. Alarums. Enter CASSIUS and TITINIUS

TITINIUS
O Cassius, Brutus gave the word too early,
Who having some advantage on Octavius,
Took it too eagerly: his soldiers fell to spoil,
Whilst we by Antony are all enclos'd.

Enter PINDARUS

PINDARUS
Fly further off my lord: fly further off,
Mark Antony is in your tents my lord:
Fly therefore noble Cassius, fly far off.

CASSIUS
This hill is far enough. Look, look, Titinius
Are those my tents where I perceive the fire?

TITINIUS
They are, my lord.

CASSIUS
Mount thou my horse, and hide thy spurs in him,
Till he have brought thee up to yonder troops
And here again, that I may rest assur'd
Whether yond troops, are friend or enemy.

TITINIUS
I will be here again.

Exit

CASSIUS
Go Pindarus, get higher on that hill,
My sight was ever thick: regard Titinius,
And tell me what thou not'st about the field.

PINDARUS ascends the hill

Sirrah, what news?

PINDARUS
[Above] O my lord.
Titinius is enclosed round about
With horsemen, that make to him on the spur,
Yet he spurs on. Now they are almost on him:
He's ta'en. And, hark, they shout for joy.

CASSIUS
O, coward that I am, to live so long,
To see my best friend ta'en before my face.
Come hither sirrah:
In Parthia did I take thee prisoner,
And then I swore thee, saving of thy life,
That whatsoever I did bid thee do,
Thou shouldst attempt it. Come now, keep thine oath,
Now be a freeman, and with this good sword,

That ran through Caesar's bowels, search this bosom.
Stand not to answer: here, take thou the hilts,
And when my face is cover'd, as 'tis now,
Guide thou the sword.

PINDARUS stabs him

Caesar, thou art reveng'd,
Even with the sword that kill'd thee.

Dies

PINDARUS
So, I am free;
Yet would not so have been,
Durst I have done my will. O Cassius,
Far from this country Pindarus shall run,
Where never Roman shall take note of him.

Exit. Re-enter TITINIUS with MESSALA

MESSALA
It is but change, Titinius: for Octavius
Is overthrown by noble Brutus' power,
As Cassius' legions are by Antony.

TITINIUS
These tidings will well comfort Cassius.

MESSALA
Is not that he that lies upon the ground?

TITINIUS
O setting sun: as in thy red rays thou dost sink to night;
So in his red blood Cassius' day is set.

The sun of Rome is set.
Our day is gone, our deeds are done.

MESSALA
O hateful error, melancholy's child:
Why dost thou show to the apt thoughts of men
The things that are not?
I go to meet the noble Brutus,
Thrusting this report into his ears;
Piercing steel and darts envenomed,
Shall be as welcome to the ears of Brutus,
As tidings of this sight.

Exit MESSALA

TITINIUS
Why didst thou send me forth, brave Cassius?
Did I not meet thy friends, and did not they
Put on my brows the wreath of victory,
And bid me give it thee? Didst thou not hear their shouts?
Alas, thou hast misconstrued every thing.
Brutus, come apace, and see how I regarded Caius Cassius.
By your leave gods: this is a Roman's part,
Come Cassius' sword, and find Titinius' heart.

*Kills himself. Alarum. Re-enter MESSALA, BRUTUS, CATO,
STRATO and VOLUMNIUS*

BRUTUS
Where, where, Messala, doth his body lie?

MESSALA
Lo yonder, and Titinius mourning it.

BRUTUS
Titinius' face is upward.

CATO
He is slain.

BRUTUS
O Julius Caesar, thou art mighty yet!
Thy spirit walks abroad and turns our swords
In our own proper entrails.
Friends I owe more tears
To this dead man, than you shall see me pay.
I shall find time, Cassius: I shall find time.
Come, therefore, and to Thasos send his body.
The ghost of Caesar hath appear'd to me
Two several times by night; at Sardis once,
And, this last night, here in Philippi fields:
I know my hour is come.

VOLUMNIUS
Not so, my lord.

BRUTUS
Nay, I am sure it is.
Thou seest the world, Volumnius, how it goes,
Our enemies have beat us to the pit:
It is more worthy, to leap in ourselves,
Than tarry till they push us.

Alarum

Countrymen: my heart doth joy that yet in all my life,
I found no man, but he was true to me.
I shall have glory by this losing day
More than Octavius, and Mark Antony,
By this vile conquest shall attain unto.
So fare you well at once, for Brutus' tongue
Hath almost ended his life's history:
Night hangs upon mine eyes, my bones would rest,
That have but labour'd, to attain this hour.

Alarum

Hence: farewell, I will follow.

Exeunt all but BRUTUS and STRATO

I prithee, Strato, stay thou by thy lord,
Thou art a fellow of a good respect:
Hold then my sword, and turn away thy face,
While I do run upon it. Wilt thou Strato?

STRATO
Give me your hand first. Fare you well, my lord.

BRUTUS
Farewell good Strato.

Runs on his sword

Caesar, now be still,
I kill'd not thee with half so good a will.

Dies. Alarum. Enter OCTAVIUS, STRATO, ANTONY and MESSALA

MESSALA
Strato, where is thy master?

STRATO
Free from the bondage you are in, Messala,
The conquerors can but make a fire of him:
For Brutus only overcame himself,
And no man else hath honour by his death.

OCTAVIUS
All that served Brutus, I will entertain them.

MESSALA
How died my master Strato?

STRATO
I held the sword, and he did run on it.

MESSALA
Octavius, then take him to follow thee,
That did the latest service to my master.

ANTONY
This was the noblest Roman of them all:
All the conspirators save only he,
Did that they did, in envy of great Caesar:
He only, in a general honest thought,
And common good to all, made one of them.
His life was gentle, and the elements
So mix'd in him, that nature might stand up,
And say to all the world: 'This was a man.'

OCTAVIUS
According to his virtue, let us use him
With all respect, and rites of burial.
Within my tent his bones tonight shall lie,
Most like a soldier order'd honourably:
So call the field to rest, and let's away,
To part the glories of this happy day.

Exeunt

NOTES

Specifically abridged to create one-hour performance scripts that maintain the essential elements needed for an introduction to three of Shakespeare's greatest histories.

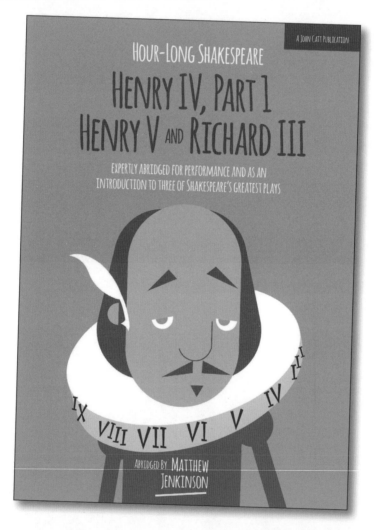

Also available from www.johncattbookshop.com